Walking Through Shadows

Walking Through Shadows

A JOURNEY OF LOSS AND RENEWAL

MIKE CAWTHORNE

BIRLINN

First published in 2019 by Birlinn Ltd
West Newington House
10 Newington Road
Edinburgh
EH9 1QS

www.birlinn.co.uk

ISBN: 978 1 78027 603 8

British Library Cataloguing in Publication Data
A catalogue record for this book is available from the British Library

Typeset by Initial Typesetting Services, Edinburgh
Printed and bound by Gutenberg Press Ltd, Malta

Contents

Illustrations

Camp on the north coast at the beginning of our walk, Tongue Bay in the distance.

Descending Ben Hutig.

Approaching Ben Hee from the east.

Crossing the Allt na Claise Moire.

At the head of Loch a' Ghriama and a distant Loch Shin.

Afternoon shadows on the climb to the hills of the Cassley Basin.

A perishing morning in the Assynt Basin.

The ruin of Tubeg, by Loch Assynt and Quinag.

Leaving Suilven and heading south-east.

Loch Gorm and Creag Dubh a' Gorm Locha in the Fannichs.

Sunrise on Sgurr a'Bhealaich Dheirg. A view from Camban bothy.

Waterfall in Coire Chorsalain.

Looking down Loch Hourn to Ladhar Bheinn and Barrisdale Bay.

A last descent east along Loch Hourn to our final camp.

Ladhar Beinn from the north shore of Loch Hourn.

Clive on the summit of Beinn a' Chreachain, April 2012.

For Anne

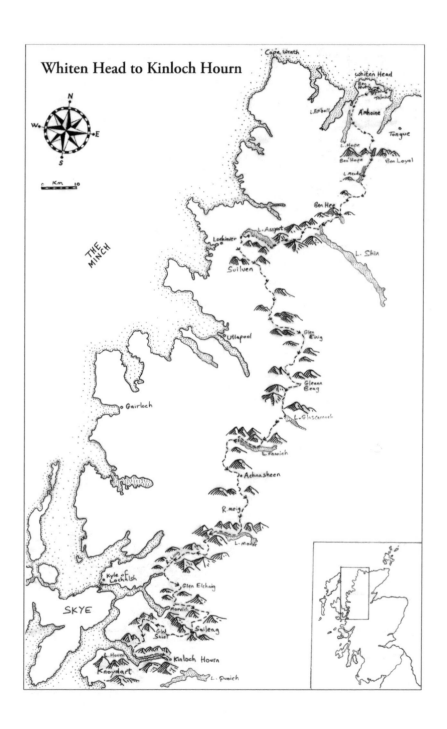

Whiten Head to Kinloch Hourn

N
W E
S

c. Km 10

Cape Wrath

Whiten Head
Ben
Hope
Talmine
A'mhoine

L. Eriboll

Tongue

L. Hope
Ben Hope
Ben Loyal

L. meadie

THE
MINCH

Ben Hee

L. Assynt
Lochinver

L. Shin

Suilven

Glen
Einig

Ullapool

Gleann
Beag

Gairloch

L. Glascarnoch

L. Fannich

Achnasheen

R. meig

L. monar

Kyle of
Lochalsh

Glen Elchaig

morvic

Saileag

SKYE

Glen
Shiel

L. Hourn
Kinloch Hourn

Knoydart

L. Quoich

One

When we left the road and stepped onto the moor the wind came on more strongly. As if it had been lying in wait. It had blown the snow into small drifts on the switchback trail, the way leading north then west, taking the lie of the land as we climbed gradually onto the deserted cape. A jagged coastline stretched out behind, a pale valance of surf against the dark cliffs and skerries of Tongue Bay. To the south the ground sloped and gathered in folds of grey snow, rose and dipped and rose again at the last to a hill of turrets and towers, Ben Loyal. Like the relic of some great wall built long ago against the night.

Cattle in their varied livery stood waiting for dusk and watched us pass. In the middle distance a group of deer on the run, for seconds their shapes clear against the snow before they passed into dark. Their silent hoof-beats stolen by the wind. Only the sound of rushing water was company to us that first hour, coming and fading on the breeze. That and the scratch of our pole plants, the tramp of each upward step, consoling and marking time at the beginning of our journey.

Nick was a few yards behind and when I stopped he did like-wise. There was something by the track. A torn piece of timber that appeared to have belonged once to a small boat. Some terrible force had rent it from its fixings and carried it here. A few days ago a great storm had crossed northern Scotland and in the community minibus earlier we'd passed ranks of upturned pines, outbuildings open to the sky, phone wires slack and tangled like strange knitting. In the days and weeks to come we would see other reminders, or messages if we would care to read them. The storm had flattened much and it would have flattened our tents.

Nick looked at the wreckage but I'm not sure if he made the connection. In addition to his meticulously packed sac that pulled at his broad shoulders he bore a kind of dead weight, some sense of detachment from the things about. We walked on. Snow covered the ruts of the track and filled the ditch beside it, but we could easily make out its line over the moor and after a while and at nowhere in particular I pulled up and turned to speak to Nick. Growing dark and we needed a sheltered place to spend the next seventeen hours, the extent of a winter's night in these parts. There was a burn away to our left. It had eaten down into the hillside and I hoped it might hold a terrace large enough for two small tents so we went to look. When we got there the ground sloped and it took a while to get our pitches right, fussing over the guys and sinking our axes for vestibule anchors. High banks shielded us from all but the northwest. Nothing though could be done about a night spate.

A chill damp was around me as soon as I stopped working. At the cusp of a vast entity of ocean it reminded me that coastal cold was worse even than that of the mountains, and the cold of the north coast worst of all. I wriggled into my bag and boiled water and called to Nick when it was done. All but dark. I lay back and closed my eyes and listened to the flapping fly and let the noise of the burn in again. Clearer notes now, a mild clucking within a few deeper sounds, like a shallow pot filling and overflowing.

I thought of all the sounds people sleep to, here was some-thing better even than silence. Was the sound of a burn the last sound to reach him, I wondered now as I'd wondered many times? What had called him to that ledge or such a place where frozen runoff made a treachery of each step? A wink of water under the ice that pulsed like newborn life in a membrane, a thing so fragile yet shelled around by the earth and this part so unyielding.

When I awoke and looked out a bright rosy band lay to the southeast. It promised much for our first full day and I said so to Nick.

'If that's my alarm call then you're too late,' he said. 'I've been awake for a while.' He looked up at me from his vestibule, a little dishevelled, his hair matted.

'Doing what?'

'Listening to the breeze, thinking.'

'You putting in a little practice for the nights ahead?'

'What d'you mean by that?'

'I mean time, we're going to have plenty. If this thing works out. A small matter that. I'm guessing you've a book, something to read?'

He rooted about inside. A palm-sized box with buttons and dials. A thin wire trailed from its side. He held it up.

'No book, just a listening device. For music. Time away in the hills doesn't mean I should deprive myself.'

'You make it sound like a penance. It might have been nice to leave modern life at home for once.'

'I've also a load of lectures to listen to, you know for my Masters.'

'Conservation and ecology?'

Nick nodded.

'That does sound like a penance.'

Great silver-edged clouds floated over the sea as we slowly packed, bursts of sun on the snowy Moine. I'd never been to Whiten Head before this journey, had barely heard of it, the north-western tip of the peninsula before it plunges south to Loch Eriboll. The coast hereabouts little-known and rarely seen in detail, for no boat can land safely and few people except shepherds ever skirt the cliffs to peer into the last coves and rocky bays of Scotland. Away from the coast the land climbs quickly to a thousand feet and the brooding Ben Hutig, a familiar landmark to the Norsemen and a warning not to stray too close. Apart from a scattering of crofts and dwellings along Tongue bay the two dozen square miles of peninsula are devoid of humankind, a bare and treeless place roamed over by sheep and the chevroned trails of their keepers.

After regaining the track we could see northeast as far as the Orkney mainland and red sandstone of Hoy, a distant presence the first hours, but far greater was the expanse of sea, a stage-set marked by random pools of light and shadings where squalls fermented, growing from nothing and hurrying past and dying as if they might be just spectral winds for none ever reached us. Where we trod, though, had seen much disturbance, the snow blown into ditches whose depth we judged by rushes breaking the surface. Crossing such drifts we were often to our knees, no easy rhythm, the track long gone. We'd been slowly gaining height but the land trended north and it seemed to want to pull us towards its ring of cliffs now some way below. Here the snow was less and we stopped and for a minute considered whether to drop lower and skirt Whiten Head itself, a longer walk but the going might be easier. We stayed high.

Ben Hutig's northern arm crested our sightline and we cut up to reach it, twelve hundred feet above the ocean and offering a vantage to prospect a route west to Eriboll on the far side of the peninsula. The wind stronger here and it came at us with a great dose of interior cold. We gazed over to the ancient Moine upland and rising from this the hills of Ben Hope, Meallan Liath, Ben Loyal – bald rock faces, backlit and streaming banners of snow. At our feet the land fell steeply to a frozen loch and we dropped and crossed its outflow and tracked the miles of empty snow and climbed again to a broad moor and another loch, resting here in the lee of a bank for lunch though it was well past noon. All the ice on the loch had wind-jammed at this end and grey slabs lay heaped up like a jerry-built breakwater. Spume from wavetops flew over our heads as we crouched and made soup and supped the scalding brew and said little. In another mile the land began to drop, the snow-cover fading. We gained the coast and found ourselves teetering above a bay cradled by a half round of sheer cliffs, these displaying bands of yellowish strata and terminating in arch and stack. Something reassuring about the symmetry, I thought, as if their geological arrangement matched a page vaguely recalled from a school textbook, an old annotated photo or idealised litho. These things almost a parody. We sat on the sward and let our eyes wander and watched lines of combers break on the shingle far below and I counted the gap between their breaking and the boom reaching us. Sheep tracks ringed the steep turf but barely a sign that people ever came this way.

Nick said a place like this in the south would draw thousands. It would be on postcards and calendars and you'd know it immediately. I said I was thankful the chocolate-box marketeers hadn't been here, were probably not even aware it existed. A name on the map, nothing more. Nick regarded the scene again. He gestured with both palms, as if weighing the air. You could package it up, he said, and sell it same as everything else. Why not? It's taken a few million years to reach this state. Open it up. If you want more places protected then get folk in so they can be appreciated and loved. You can love places to death, I said.

A short way from here the sea had taken a huge bite from the land and around the next bend we saw the roof of an old house. I'd been gathering some fallen and rotting posts and strapped rather too many to my sac, crossways and skywards, and could now only walk face down with arms outstretched to act as counter. As if demonstrating some new form of locomotion. The unbalance made the last quarter mile a proper stagger.

The thick walls of the old place curbed somewhat the sound of storm that rose later that evening and ran through the night. Just before dawn I went out to see the loch streaked with white and from a headland came the crack of unseen waves and flurries of spray. Grey clouds smothered all save nearby hills and fresh snow lay to low levels. A waterfall behind the house curled uphill with every gust.

Last night's fire was but a memory, the cold now invading every receptor, and only by wrapping myself in layers was I content to sit and deal with breakfast. The draw of wind over the roof was such we agreed to prune our earlier aim of crossing the Moine direct and instead would follow the shoreline south to the hamlet of Hope and seek refuge in the woods for the night.

I was packed and ready soon after I'd eaten. Nick still had to sort his kit and began by making small piles on the bench, the table and floor. Slowly he moved items between the piles so that some grew and others shrunk. This went on for a while until he stood back and stared at the assembly with a pinched expression, as if there was a riddle to be solved. And this before he'd even stowed away his first bit of gear. The actual packing was achingly slow and accompanied by moments of quiet cursing. I sat quietly and read my book, fully aware that even the smallest comment could derail everything. I didn't once check the time, though when Nick finally pulled fast the last strap and stood up ready to go I knew hours had passed. I let him speak first. 'Sorry about that. Promise I'll get faster.'

A kind of path climbed from the rear of the house that vanished once on the moor and from this small vantage we surveyed the greater length of Loch Eriboll, the sea blistered with waves piling in from the Atlantic, their tips broken with tails of spume and all the skerries and rocks and distant shore were wrapped in skirts of spray. Billowing snow crossed the moors then all grew dark as we became engulfed, spats of white, the hill outlines gone and the visible world narrowed, the gale strong and cold enough to spin our gaze and unsettle our walking so that we measured each step and made adjustments as the wind rose and fell. At a scant shelter afforded by a kind of outcrop we hunkered down with the map. From a hidden defile ahead came gouts of foam. At first we reckoned them from onshore breakers, but in fact they were born of a river, the Allt a t-Srathain, which drains the northern Moine. Dropping to the banks we searched for an easy place to ford but there was none. I ran splashing over a dubious line of submerged boulders and got wet. Nick removed his boots and with great caution guided his feet and yelled as if river crabs were at his toes.

Cnoc nan Gobhar barred our route and rose five hundred feet from the shore, its seaward flanks horribly exposed to the gale, so we pulled from the river and climbed inland in its lee to a col near the summit, and then as we stepped over the crest a prolonged squall hit us. For seconds we reeled away and were almost uplifted. Snow danced and flew wildly. We turned and went crabwise and I could only see ahead by cupping a mittened hand to my forehead in a strange salute. Nick gestured in a kind of semaphore. He wanted to get down, he said, and it was the fastest I'd seen him move for some time as we went straight for the coast, rime now forming on heather and rocks, and we pressed on until finding a windless niche among great boulders. A place for some soup but we had no water and I thought it a waste of gas to melt snow, so we continued until there was a trickle enough for a panful and sat supping it in a hollow among wet snow and dead stalks of last year's bracken, the wind in the crags above shaped to a tuneless fluting.

Over the next rise the shoreline gathered into another

headland but before this a corridor of calmer water, the mouth of the River Hope, a short outflow draining Loch Hope, and here the driving waves broke and died as they reached the shallows. A pair of eagles rode the hills to the south, spiralling shapes against the heavens and on paths divergent until drawn together as if on unseen cords. Nick hadn't seen them when I asked.

From nowhere a path and we picked down this towards the shore and a stoutly built cottage, then a wood of stunted birch, the ground soft with old leaf-fall, and we came out at a rough track and shell of an old house, still roofed and dark inside like a bunker. We thought about sleeping here, though not seriously and stole along the river to a grove of tall native pines, swaying and creaking in the wind. Here was shelter and good ground, but also windfall. Old and bleached limbs from prior storms. Nick looked at the ground and looked up at the trees.

'What do you think?' he said.

'I think if we camp here there's a chance we might be woken in the night. Maybe not even woken.'

'Seems alright to me. I've pitched up in many a wood, in many a wind.'

I went to pick up one of the fallen branches but it wouldn't shift. Time had glued it to the ground. I looked up at the canopy.

'Some big arms up there. You wouldn't believe the weight hanging over you. They're going to come down eventually and if we camp we'd be taking a risk, though a small one, granted. A winter's night is a long time to be in the firing line. That possibility is enough to take me elsewhere.'

'The river might flood. Have you seen all this debris?'

'I don't expect it to, though. But we know there's more wind coming.'

So we set our tents amongst bracken in a clearing of small birch, pegs palmed in as the sky blackened and hail fell to whiten the old fronds and rattle the tents. I fumbled with the last guy and dived inside and sat listening to the din.

The north coast road crossed the bridge only a quarter of a mile upstream, and in the hours of lying in my bag reading and eating and talking to Nick I heard maybe three cars. A brief rise and fall of vehicular noise sounding almost alien against the thrash of wind in the canopy and grumbling of river in near spate.

I woke once during the night and amid the clatter of more hail I thought Nick might be right about the flooding. Loch Hope is a large body of water, repository of a great catchment and it could conceivably surge as we slept, no less a risk than a falling branch. I didn't think I believed in fate or luck, but rather we can weigh what factors count against and what for, and on that we proceed. Though I sometimes wonder if I might be wrong, that my freedom to choose is just another illusion. Are we compelled on paths already written, trapped in some loop of contingency, our choices no more than actions predetermined, each of us like a wind-up toy set loose on a trajectory as fixed as the orbit of planets and stars in the void of space?

I wondered if he'd set out that morning on such a course, no choice at all and no voices or the faintest premonition of what was to befall.

In this northern river valley it was nine before there was enough light to dismantle our tents by and when a squall came suddenly even that light was gone. So gloomy I almost reached for my torch. I was brushing my teeth when a lady with five dogs approached on the river path and seemed startled when she saw me. I greeted her but there was something cool in her response. Her dogs, mostly Labradors, were nonplussed by the transient residents and the whole crowd passed on and I never saw them again. I guess we probably appeared like itinerant tramps and you might wonder on our business being out all night at this time of year, in such weather. It revived a memory of some years before, when I came across a tent and two Germans huddled over a small campfire by our local river. Wandering souls both, they spoke of their journey and asked which bank might be best upstream and what obstacles human or otherwise might they encounter. Next day only a ring of stones and ashes told of their stay. I kicked the stones into the water and footed wet leaves over their fire site and in a few days couldn't say for sure even where they'd been.

When ready we turned onto the single track road that ran alongside Loch Hope. The slush covering the surface was free of tyre tracks and a sign ahead read 'Road Closed'. Showers of wet snow hurried in from the north, the hills across the water lost in fast-moving cloud. Our route from here lay over the Moine and crossed desolate country east and south of Ben Hope. Although I was wary of crossing in these conditions, at least the wind had moderated from yesterday's heights. Nick said little. I thought there was a lethargy about his movements, as if something was profoundly wrong, but when I asked he said he was fine. My pace took me ahead and I stopped next at a bridge that went over one of the hillside burns. Caught on the ironwork were clods of peat and brash and wigs of old grasses, all of it debris from a spate, and I reckoned we were today twelve feet above the tumbling waters. As we struck up for the moor and gained a vantage we looked further lochside. A whole section of road was missing. Fractured as if by some quake and carried away foundation and all, and in its place raw gravels and stripped brown earth. The road was closed because it was no longer there.

Nick struggled and now conceded he was taking a while getting used to his load. I nodded and said as much about my own, hoping it would spur him on. We crossed a high wooded burn where leafless trees were aged and dying, run through by deer, and then to the open moor, walking by compass and by any feature that broke the sameness, a gully or slope of wind-scour or drift of snow or gum of peat, anything to aim at, and we walked on steadily until finding ourselves at the very heart of the Moine. At the axle whose far orbits were no longer there. Only in the distance could we see the coast and ocean fringe carrying small spotlights of sun.

Squalls from the west telegraphed their approach and coalesced and came at us like walls of dust, the driving snow mixing with ground-drift that all but screened Nick. I waited until he appeared again. The winds passed and twice a band of light came to flood the moor and transform it into a dazzle of blue and white, and when looking around now we could reckon the way ahead. At this height the snow had smoothed the ground into a uniform cloth, a covering we trod both in ignorance and caution as many times we became snared, sinking in so deep our boots came back up with coppery mud bleeding over the snow like a strange dye.

What little progress we made was marked by the slow passing of Ben Hope. Its dark side has brooded like a totem these million years and it came and went in plumes of drift as did the spurs and butts of its satellites. We still seemed to be rising so I checked again the wavering needle of my compass and eyed the terrain. Something wasn't right. Nick reckoned the Moine was trying to entrap us, that the ghosts of early hunters and travellers who perished in the sinks here were leading us astray and on a trail only to their bones or a leathery cadaver in the peat. Through a brief opening was the snowless plain by the Tongue road, burnt brown with a scatter of pale cottages, so tiny from here, and save for those crofts and their green moats, the interior rose empty and vast, square miles without a single dwelling or anything you could identify as human, just moors and hills and grey skies to frame them.

The land trended east now and we with it on a long slow descent, though staying high in the hope of a more direct line to the track that would take us south through the hills and to a base for the night. A wind-blown shoulder of Ben Loyal appeared and we sited it with compass and walked towards it. A guiding landmark of old for those lost on the moor. At a deepset burn a shower of heavy snow strengthened the gloom and left a lethal slush on the crossing stones. The very real worry of being caught on the moor in the dark had given Nick a burst of energy, and now when I turned he was close behind, his face drawn with tiredness. I said the track was down there and pointed. We found it as darkness fell and a sleety rain came against our backs. I relaxed, but as the way began to climb again our marching grew more weary and in the dark there was nothing for my eyes nor much to think of save the growing burden of the day. I waited for Nick only once, hearing his boots on the ground through the slush, then his breathing. A vague shape ghosted into view.

'No torch?' I said.

'Nah. Can just about make things out. Is it far?'

'Close enough to see if it were daylight.'

'Like one of those toy houses we saw from up there on the moor? That's a long way.'

'Okay then, we're so close we can smell it. Well, almost.'

Nick nosed the air in mock gesture.

'Only thing I can smell is us.'

The snow lay greyly on the gorse bushes both sides of the track, and only by these forms did I know the way, now left and turning, and down there a dark mass was the unfrozen Loch na Dithreaibh. I caught a rooty smell of old planking and in another minute something grew from the earth, an outline of a gable. Four walls and a roof that claimed one small dry square from the night sleet. I turned back into the night and shouted. Nick was only a few minutes behind and by the time he showed I was inside with my stove out and was heating water. We unwrapped tents to air, tying them to fixings so they hung in great folds and glistened in the candlelight, Nick a little fore of these curtains settled to cook, hunching over and eying what simmered in his pot, so still he looked in deep meditation. I thought if he could sleep that way he would. He blinked and very deliberately took a spoon and began to stir. Later in the warmth of our bags with yet another drink we both felt a little revived and could speak more easily. Nick asked about our route.

'Most journeys in the Highlands finish at a settlement or the coast and maybe a few on a hilltop if climbing summits is what you're doing,' I said, 'I want to finish where Clive was eventually found, in Knoydart, so when thinking about a route at least I knew our destination.'

'What was your idea? Though I guess I'll be finding out soon enough.'

'I remember reading something about how reindeer in Scandinavia purposely avoid human stuff, be it houses, roads, dams, wind farms or whatever. The health of the herd is reliant on corridors of untamed land along which they can migrate. That's true of most wild creatures. So I wondered if there were still left in Scotland a line from the north that was just that. Did it exist, could we find it?'

Nick sipped from his mug that was brim-full and steaming.

'I think we're going to struggle,' he said. 'And anyway, much of the land is only wild in your perception. The old forests and great beasts that once lived in them are gone. Man's influence is everywhere. Only the ignorant can't see that. Our sense of the wild is a modern construct and I'll wager it largely comes from an urban mindset. It's about appearances, where there are few if any signs of alteration, as if the land had always been this way. That's pretty naïve.'

'Maybe, but there are still big tracts out there, albeit reduced to grouse moor or heavily grazed by deer. Places where you don't see turbines, even from a distance, or a loch troubled by concrete and metal. And I'd like to find the last woods in the west. By putting together previous experiences of these places and what I've read and stuff folk have told me I've settled on a route of sorts.'

'One that crosses roads and sometimes use tracks and paths.'

'Yep, no getting away from that.'

'Can you show me the line?'

'On a map?'

'Of course.'

'Not really. It's in my head. Well, sort of. We have to reach our caches, but that aside the route is not fixed like some long distance way, though it helps those at home to know where we are. The caches only mark our road crossings. They give a framework. The detail is up to us.'

'Like stopping here.' Nick looked around at the bare interior. 'That kind of detail I appreciate.'

'Yeah, this roof is handy, particularly on such a night.'

'Man-made though. Shouldn't we be camping?'

'Humans have always been a part of the wild but I like the thought that we just pass through and leave it to the creatures that make their lives here. They rely on it. Maybe in the future this line and others like it could become a restored corridor of native trees and free-running rivers. Who knows. Perhaps someday reindeer will be using it.'

The window on the north side clattered with an onslaught of hailstones. Our candle trembled.

We spoke of our friend and maybe the real reason why we were there.

'This walk is for his memory, a kind of homage,' I said. 'And I want to do it his way. His time in the hills wasn't about accumulating daily mileages or climbing particular peaks. He enjoyed nothing more than to wander from place to place. Just poking about old woods or sitting waiting for an otter or wave-watching. He simply loved wild places.'

'Clive never went on long walks.'

'No, but he always had the travel bug. Even when living in Inverness he went abroad for his hols, mostly on his own and always backpacking. He was single. Work was his passion but he liked to get away. He passed hundreds of days in the hills, mind, in fact I would say latterly they became a more important part of his life. Sleeping out was his thing. He never owned a tent. And he did sometimes talk of doing a long walk, over a few weeks at least.'

'So this could have been his?'

'Yes. I thought about that when planning our general route. Clive loved places where nature was in charge and believe it or not he also loved rough weather. Maybe not a full-on blizzard but certainly a big wind to stir up the sea or rain that turns rivers to torrents. He embraced such conditions. Maybe in the end that was his undoing.'

Nick was quiet for a minute. Sleet was being driven against the window. He looked over to the noise. 'Do you think we're going to get hammered?' he said.

The long night was troubled by winds that went ratcheting

up and fell abruptly and in the lulls I heard waves along the shore and hail periodically lancing the roof. By first light a few more inches of snow had fallen, and when out for water I had to break ice on the river. As I came back with numbed fingers the sky darkened and a squall gathered over the loch like a great drift of loess. The hills disappeared and we break-fasted by torchlight. Hailstones drowned our small-talk, but there wasn't much to talk about in any case. We needed to reach our first food cache by nightfall, that was all. Nick sprinkled coconut powder and sultanas over his porridge. After packing I made a second brew and spread three map sheets onto the floor, as the day's route took us across the perimeter of each. For some time I studied the maps, then drifted to reading my book as Nick continued the glacial process of assembling his kit, the collating of piles, the careful placing of each in his sac. The fifth morning he'd done so, but I noticed he showed lit-tle familiarity with the routine, as if it was the first time he'd done it.

Outside the day was already advanced. We set out south by west, the first hour bright, the sun lifting the snow to ribbons of brilliance that made us squint, but such light disappeared soon enough and the snow became grey and without depth and the only colour anywhere was a green understory of gorse that colo-nised the track verge in some profusion. Our way left the flats at the head of the loch and climbed until we looked down onto the river looping sad and scattered relics of birch, as if their seed were barren all these years. On the far side of the valley the land was steep and it broke sometimes into crags or a spur truncated, dark against the snow, and one having the likeness of a human face, etched into a frown.

Scanning the snow ahead, I broke trail and thought hard about my line. I paused at intervals and turned to see if Nick matched my steps, thereby saving himself, if only a little. I knew my stride was a little longer than his so I made adjustments and hoped that would help. When I asked he said my pacing was okay but also said that as he was heavier there was sometimes no advantage in following, so he would make his own trail and for me not to worry. In the days to come I would occasionally fall back and follow him and came to realise his meandering lines of heavy prints carried another message.

I thought of our very first trip together when we'd also walked through snow, but more I recalled how we'd prepared for it. He was new to the hills and in need of proper kit. For Nick the boggling array of options proved a bigger hurdle than the later snow peaks. For each item he weighed my advice and dithered and with each purchase came lingering doubts. Had he made the right choice?

The ripples from a poor equipment choice will fade but when Nick came to see me in Scotland he fell in love with my friend. She moved back to her native Canada, he followed, swapping his teaching job and a steady income for adventure and uncertainty. They married, travelled and trekked in the Yukon, laboured on farms, settling in a small resort high in the Rockies. She managed the campground, Nick wrote a fantasy novel and explored the wilderness, often alone and in winter. The grizzlies were all asleep then, he said. There was solace here but tensions as well and the couple left the mountains, coming eventually back to Scotland. She worked, he couldn't. For Nick even journeys into the hills had became fraught. He spoke of being unable to leave a bothy once for four days, the walls closing in and the imaginary moat outside filled with fear. Next spring she left and never returned. That was five years ago.

The light was greying and when Nick crunched up beside me he didn't stop. The river narrowed and lessened until close to the watershed we stepped over it and approached the dark shape of Loch Meadie, the snow here half a foot or more. A bitter wind blowing downcountry now and the hills around shrinking to a grey gauze, then a vanguard of dancing snowflakes, waves driven against our shore. We wanted to stop for soup but there was no shelter, not the least place beyond the wind's reach. The lying snow had no base and that falling was beginning to drift and in a very short time new deposits lay over old and it was hard to know where to tread.

At around mid-afternoon the light began to go, the loch-side bleaker, a sense hardly softened by the first of a series of small wooded isles. Something to count against the distance. Windbent trees and the failing day. We walked into darkness and could just see the last of the isles telling us the loch hadn't far to run, but it was a lie.

When fully dark the wind seemed to come at us all the stronger and blew snow across our torch-beams in blinding sparks so we were forced to walk bent as neither of us had any eye protection. No place to stop even if we'd wanted to. Nick was noticeably tiring. We hardly saw the loch now, in fact we purposely avoided it. There was no wisdom in using its shore as a handrail which in any case would be ill-defined and a matter of guesswork this wet season, and even if the shore existed as the map claimed, I reckoned at this nether end it would jag about too much and double the distance remaining.

Nick pointed to his feet. A little sore, he said, and could we stop. No shelter here, I said. I don't need shelter just rest. And he sat on a stone right there with his back to the wind and hunched and almost seemed to rock. I crouched beside him and waited, the snow coming in small hard pellets, thwacking our hoods and dizzying away.

The line of the road was unmistakable. Drifted over in places, there was not the slightest mark any vehicle had driven here for days and we spent time locating the rubble pile that concealed our food, the snow-cover at first tricking the memory and obliterating our marker.

Going south along the road the wind eased and with it the snow. Facing us if we could see it was the great bowl of the Meadie and Mundale rivers but we saw nothing beyond our sawing beams, not the smallest mote of light from a lived-in house nor even a star in the heavens, as if we had over us some dark cloak from which there was no escape. For more than an hour we lifted our boots over the drifted snow, then at an old plantation felled years before turned west, and went as far as a broad noisy burn and here made camp.

In late evening the night opened to a fretwork of embers burning in their millions but the hard frost had me sinking further into my sleeping bag. When I looked out again it was breaking day. The first rosy glow and a wider landscape, Ben Kilbreck a shadowed blue wall, Ben Hope in saffron. I got into my boots and squeaked about the snow. I thumped my hands to keep them from freezing and looked over at Nick's tent. In the frozen gravel he'd had difficulty placing his pegs and now his guys were slack and his outer sheet white and weighed down with hoar. It was hard to believe anyone was inside. A shifting sound and the sound of a blister pack being squeezed open and water being drunk. A small voice and it betrayed much tiredness.

Nick went through his rituals of assembly. I stayed warm by pacing some distance away until with the sun at its meridian and all shadows extending north we removed our boots and socks and waded the icy waters and headed west. The curve of our chosen path clearly seen if not so easily followed as each step went in nearly a foot, and it quickly dawned that crossing the watershed east of Ben Hee was the most we could wish for that day. I broke trail, Nick emulating my steps, more carefully than yesterday I thought. Our world opened to an arena of solitary hills, Ben Hope, Loyal, Stumanadh, Kilbreck all ranged north to east in brittle clarity, and at that quarter in the blue distance a pair of beckoning tops that I thought were Ben Armine and Creag Mhor. If there was any movement anywhere we missed it, no winged creature or lumbering plane crossing our sky and the miles of vacant moor as still as if time itself had frozen. The only noise coming to us was the run of a burn a straight mile away and our own soft breathing as we went slowly upwards. A large cat, feral or wild, had already taken this path and we followed its pad marks until they veered to the headwaters of the Mundale river, perhaps chasing scent of creatures who gravitate to what open water there was. On a mound blown nearly clear of snow a group of hungry deer were using their hooves to get at the thin grasses. Barely one paused to eye us past.

As the cover thickened we began losing the path. Burns crossing our course were taken with caution, the drifted snow now covering every obstacle and there was mostly no base to any of it. Against the clear sky was the lovely curve of Ben Hee's summit dome, drawing us like latter-day pilgrims, yet it would remain untrodden, and often does for weeks at a time, for winter travellers are few. In the days to come and for as long as snow lay on the ground ours were the only human marks we saw.

Climbing into afternoon's shadow we laboured somewhat, our boots catching all facets of buried rock and at one place my leg went down and hung swinging over some void or sunken channel. These hidden sinks were the land's greatest deception. We could usually read the dangers but usually is not always and I reckoned there was no greater hazard to a wanderer of these parts.

At Bad a' Bhacaich and at our highest point we blinked at the dying sun and from the dyke-work of an old cairn looked over to Ben Hee, its blue corrie and frozen seeps, and below us the grey frozen loch of the watershed winding to its egress. As the last shadows faded we tackled two miles of drifts to the waters of Loch a' Ghorm-choire. I scouted for some level ground but there was none, all land sloping to the loch. Nick arrived in the last of the light and considered if we should pitch west of the loch's outflow and so avoid being marooned by a sudden thaw, but the ground there was even steeper and in any case no thaw was forecast. Indeed it would get colder. In a hurry we marked out plots and footed them to a kind of tent-shape. I scraped away the snow to bare heather and got my tent up, then cut blocks of frozen crust to fashion a sort of parapet against what I judged the prevailing winds of the country. Nick merely set his tent on a small square of flattened snow and went inside.

Dark had fallen yet the corrie retained a strange dull glow, sufficient to see by, and gathering up all our pans and bottles I went for water, kicking steps and dropping six foot to a burn channel and plunging in a bare hand and bottle and wincing on my return. Setting a pan to boil I went to the edge of the loch. Only one reach of it still free of ice and as I approached a white-breasted dipper launched over the dark surface like a thing flung by catapult. Cliffs on the far side leaked with frozen runoff and each icy runnel still holding a slight gleam from the faded day, that or an outrider of stars, I was not sure. I shivered. My breath smoked. A polar cold was about the place.

'What you doing out there?'

'Nothing.'

'I can hear you pacing about. You lost something?'

'You may be right with that. How are those feet?'

'Tad swollen I'd say.'

'You should pack them in ice.'

'Are you serious?'

'Plenty of it about, case you hadn't noticed.'

'You really don't think I'm going to last the distance, do you?'

I looked at the trodden snow outside his tent.

'I didn't mean that. It's just a bit early for those pads of yours to be giving up. We've another five weeks and I can't promise it'll get any easier.'

Nick didn't reply but we spoke of other things, of home and his girlfriend and those he missed. But he loved being here and though inside and cocooned in his layers he said he could yet feel the space of the loch and weight of hill behind and thought it special.

'What a place. Clive would have loved it.'

'Yes, he would.'

About to zip myself in for the night I noticed a shrew in my vestibule gathering crumbs and scrapings of the night's pasta. Caught in my light it lifted its little nose to sniff and cast about before carrying on with its work, if anything more determinedly than before. I lay back and listened, tiny claws on metal, something being dragged. Clive would have loved that too.

In the college library early in my first term was this guy reading a magazine, wide-rimmed glasses, hair unkempt, jersey too large for his skinny frame. I'd opened a book on Stalin, the subject of my next essay. Clive looked at the book and grinned. His first words are gone and I thought he was some kind of mentor to help first-years settle but he wasn't. He said you should come climbing, or at least sign up for a hill-walk, and as if by way of promotion launched into accounts of prior trips, a climb on Ben Nevis ending at midnight, a storm-induced crawl on a Lakeland fell, canoeing and capsizing on Loch Lomond. Up until that point in my late teens the hills had been a lonely enterprise.

Here was the promise of company so I joined, and true to his word unfolded the scrapes and close-shaves, hard miles in hard weather. Driving through the night and dawn blood-red over Kintail. Clive wasn't a good climber, wasn't especially fit. He spent his money on records rather than quality gear, but no one who met him ever forgot him. My first year was Clive's last and he left to study journalism. We kept a correspondence so I know in the next two decades he travelled and made his posts and residences bright points on the map of Britain. I only realised later how much of the colour he'd filled in.

Two

My night's breathing frosted the inner and by morning the slightest touch brought down a shower of crystals. I began thawing ice in my pan for tea and called to Nick. He'd been awake for a while he said, dozing with his headphones. Music from a band I'd never heard of.

When I went out for a first look the sky was grey and heavy and cloud covered much of the mountain. A bitter breeze came over the corrie loch, now frozen in its entirety. The ground I'd cleared for my tent had set hard around the pegs and when the time came to pack I had to lever each out, our tents too so stiff with frost they were folded like lengths of cardboard and strapped to our sacs.

I don't believe the temperature had risen a single degree by the time we crossed ice-plated rocks at the loch's outflow and traversed the steepness of Ben Hee's southern terrain, the slopes here corrugated and much broken with stones and outcrops. Downvalley was Loch Fiag and beyond it dark blocks of conifers and in the remote distance some turbines set on a hill. No houses in any place that we could see. Ashen clouds over the frozen land and no sun nor prospect of any and an eastbound wind always on our faces making it feel colder still.

The drifts on this side slowed us greatly. Nowhere was the going simple. We were always surprised when the surface crust held us and walked as if by levitating, at least until we crashed through to a soft underbelly. This grey place a changed world after yesterday's sun. A small number of deer against the frozen loch watched us pass. I knew the burn feeding the loch from the northwest can often be in spate and impassable, but its flow today was much reduced and our crossing trouble-free. We traced an offshoot of the main channel, gaining height slowly as the afternoon dimmed. By a weathered peat bank in lee of the wind I made soup and had it ready for Nick when he lumbered into view, his face brightening when I passed him the mug.

'Croutons in them?' he said, looking at the steaming broth.

'Yep, the ones with the herbs.'

'We can use mine next time.'

'What have you got left?'

'Garlic, I think.'

'No worries.'

He removed his gloves and cradled the mug and sipped and lay his head back against the snow and closed his eyes.

A while later on the side of a desolate hill called Meallan liath Beag and through a small window in the mist we saw something of the quartz and limestone peaks of Assynt, the shifting cloud presenting their scale as such I couldn't imagine our being on their slopes in just two days. It didn't seem possible.

The valley below had long been hidden but now opened up as we dropped, Loch Merkland in its glacial trench and on the Lairg-Laxford Bridge road an occasional car-light in the murk. The slope grew steeper but at least gravity helped us with the drifts and I bounced down knowing we would soon be at camp. Nick followed with his usual caution, probing with each pole and picking his own line and we reached the deserted road close to the grounds of Markland Lodge. A few hundred yards further on we crossed a footbridge over the river and entered an enclosure of saplings and scouted about for a pitch site. Under the snow thick crowns of dead grass, but a tired traveller can sleep anywhere so without much regard we trod a space and made fast our tents and straightaway got into our bags, for the cold in this valley was the most perishing yet.

After a shared meal I nursed a brew and joined the two maps to get some handle on our route west. Given our slowness I was uneasy about the next days. Our protracted mornings were a real problem. With a change in the weather brewing we needed to find a way through the hills and cross the great basin of upper Glen Cassley and then over a pass on Ben More Assynt to reach the hamlet of Inchnadamph. An empty region few enter and almost never in winter and especially with the land so locked in snow. No other way for us, though. I studied the map. The hills guarding the basin present a fortress against travellers but also a confinement, the rivers and lochs here a collecting ground for all waters in this catchment and during times of spate the lochs overflow one to the other and the rivers bulge and haemorrhage and there's no safe way, indeed you can find yourself marooned between mazy and flooding channels. With such a quantity of snow and ice even a slight amelioration would send a deluge down the Cassley. But I also knew we couldn't delay our journey west. To combat the late cold we'd eaten down our supplies and now had rations for two days, if that. With these thoughts I didn't trouble Nick though he was lying in his bag a few yards away and we could talk in the windless quiet without raising our voices.

'Lights off,' he whispered. 'Somebody's out there.'

He claimed he'd seen a flashlight in the trees. I looked through a crack in my vestibule. The land and sky almost entirely black. I wondered why our first reaction was to hunker down and hide like foxes. We were quiet for a minute.

'You reckon someone's coming to investigate us?' I said. 'Let them, what harm are we doing?'

'Maybe they think we're having a session.'

'What?'

'You know, booze.'

'This is a long way to come for a session. Where's the nearest off off-licence?'

'Also we're camped by a river.'

'We like to camp by rivers. So?'

'Yes we do, but you know how precious they can be about their rivers. Poaching and all that.'

'Wish they were just as precious about their land. Then maybe then they wouldn't always be trashing it.'

There was no light and no noise, not of boots over the snow nor hardly even that of passing traffic. We were close to a main arterial route but an hour could elapse between cars. Later I heard a vehicle slow and stop but it had done that only to allow an oncoming one to pass.

In early morning dark the windless cold conspired against any inclination to rouse and be away. Nick's tent in my torch-light sparkled with frost. I called over, but softly, the dawn so fragile I thought it wrong to speak a loud word. Away to the southwest the crown of Ben More Assynt was touched with pink and clear sky peered through breaks in the cloud. The day promised much. Nick knew we needed an early start but that knowledge was only another burden. His packing ritual was all the more involved as for this journey he'd exchanged his simple old backpack for a fresh design. Each shoulder strap now had a large carrying pouch sewn onto it, like a pair of panniers. By keeping these filled, he said, you were spreading the overall load. Well, that was the theory. He insisted it was by far the most comfortable sac he'd ever carried. But it did present him every morning with more choices, and choices were problematic.

I waited, listening to shuffling noises, of zips and fabric being folded. The great vexing questions of which items were best suited to the pouches and which went elsewhere and in what order. As I waited I thought to ask if he might pack the same as yesterday but I didn't.

I could judge the time from shadows on the hills and guessed it was almost noon as we climbed a faded path above our pitch into Coire Gorm, the snow here largely undrifted but thickening as we reached the upper corrie and by then we were wading and our progress gradual. We stopped to look back and down to Loch a' Ghriama, an offshoot of Loch Shin and frozen save a diamond-shaped lead of open water. We looked to the face of the hill across the corrie, it presenting much bare and cloven rock in whose gaps were skeletal trees, birch I reckoned, and the first we'd seen in three days of barren going.

By now the clouds had fully broken and we climbed with the sun and our own swaying shadows that in the silence wheezed, and we seemed the one thing wayward in that resplendent world. I pointed to the gleaming dome of Ben Hee and the jumble of north-reaching hills, Arkle and Foinaven shaped there against a flawless sky. Despite these and other landmarks the near ground was hard to read. Hidden boulders and troughs and deep drifts and snow halfway to our thighs and channels of running water, bullying and guiding us. Looking back over our prints, I could see we'd rarely made the shortest route between two points.

Trails of tiny and almost weightless creatures were everywhere, though as we rounded a lochan its carpet lay without blemish, as if all life-forms knew of beauty and their little hearts ran with their own enchantment. By a half-stilled waterfall we climbed over shelves of marbled ice, and the sound of small waters still flowing was the only sound. It faded as we reached a kind of tableland. To the west a pair of sizeable lochans, then the great shadowed headwall of Meallan a' Chuail, highest summit of these parts, and we ploughed on until by the frozen outflow of another loch we stopped and rested in the late sun and boiled water and ate generously of our supplies.

A mountain wall in the west now came into view, a line of peaks whose high passes between were the only ways to the coastal grounds of Assynt. The sun nearly gone behind the tallest of these, Ben More, and minute by minute their slopes darkening to silhouette. We turned and for more than a mile went due south, the valley running away to shadow, but we bent around opposite below some crags and began a fraught descent to the great basin whose iced lochs across its floorage were now like grey shards. Despite the westernmost of these lochs being just a few miles from an Atlantic sealoch, all the waters here ran southeast down the levels and into the River Cassley, eventually mingling with saline and tides far away at Bonar Bridge on the east coast.

A soft light left the high crests and brightness soaked away to an indigo hue as detail slowly congealed. We followed hoof-marks and scat of a deer trail where they had walked orderly in single file until each hoof fanned away as if the herd had been spooked or perhaps routed by the ghost of creatures who once roamed here and not so long ago. The terrain and effort to overcome it were troubling. When still about two miles from the basin floor and now almost dark we latched onto a burn and reckoned this as our guide. It had eaten into the earth and meandered in a corridor of its own making and turned a corner to fall sheer over a shelf where grew a single stunted rowan. Venus appeared, then a delicate crescent moon and later a vanguard of stars, Orion, Sirius, Auriga, all to the south, and behind us Cassiopeia and Ursa Major, the Great Bear, tethered to the bright point of Polaris. For a while we depended on such light but in the end and to stop our stumbles and keep in touch resorted to torchbeam.

Our burn groped for a way and turned in on itself as if lost, in no hurry to reach the basin. Not lost, only chiming with the land here, the strange hydrology rendering the moorland a laby-rinth of channels, all drifted over and none simple to cross and some deep enough to swallow us entire, our narrow lightshafts catching their overhangs in garish white and in the depths of one we couldn't puzzle how to climb out so traced its loopings into the moor to a point where we kicked and kneed a trench, up to our chests in blown snow. Hearing the burn again we ploughed over to it and held to its bank until a different sound reaching us was that of a broader river running shallow. The deep cold of late had tamed it to a transparency. We crossed easily and there on the far bank that seemed more or less level I began clearing away a foot of snow. After a notional regard of terrain Nick chose a site and proceeded to foot-stomp in a slow rotation, around and around, as if some ritual for an untroubled sleep. When inside he didn't venture out again. We cooked our own meals and withdrew into our shells like reptiles and little in the way of words crossed the small space between us. Just keeping warm was enough. With our exits from the world the only sound was the grumbling of water and Nick's gentle snoring which I thought plenty commentary on the day.

I went out just once at a late and unknown hour to gaze at the firmament, more stars than I could ever remember and their numbers beyond any earthbound ledger and in any case such logging would be futile and their nightly reckoning by telescopic eyes only vanity. Odd that we pass judgment on the skies yet are the only creature to soil its own nest, to the extent we are now looking to the heavens for a new world and a new nest.

Our encampment a thousand feet up promised to be a nightly sink for all the cold cradled by these hills and so it was, the most bitter of our seven nights. I'd taken the precaution of wrapping myself in extra clothes, my monkey cape on and my bivy sack fully zipped over me and only then could I sleep though if the night grew any colder I would not.

By first light the surface of my bivy was hoared in frost as were the tent's walls which sagged inwards so my tent felt even smaller.

I turned my head and called out.

'Anyone alive in there?'

The nearby river chuckled but otherwise the silence was complete.

'Nick.'

Still no answer. I thought he might have gone for a walk. I heated my boots over the stove sufficient so I could slip them on without too much grunting and stepped outside. Pink reefs of cloud over the Cassley Basin. The river had grown a fresh skin of ice. Each inhaled breath seemed to touch a wire in my nostril. There were no new footprints by Nick's tent so I spoke his name again, much louder. His voice was deeply muffled, as if he were speaking through his hand.

'Yeah, just a second, I'll take these off. I was miles away.'

'A lecture?'

'That's right, one about habitat succession.'

'That should keep your mind off the present.'

'It's not really about that, though I probably do overthink things.'

'I thought you'd gone deaf, or maybe for a walk.'

'A walk? Here? I won't be going an inch further than I have to today. This snow is seriously hard work. In case you hadn't noticed.'

'It might get a lot harder, I mean, to walk in.'

'What d'you mean?'

'I mean there's a thaw coming.'

'When?'

'Later today, probably this afternoon. At any rate by tomorrow there's going to be an almighty flood right here.'

Nick was quiet for a moment.

'Well,' he said, 'having seen it like this I wouldn't want to see it all soggy and black. We need to get on.'

'You said it.'

I didn't think we would, though. Perhaps the sheer frigidity slowed his morning routine, if routine it was, but in my head I expected the morning to be gone by the time we broke camp. I packed and stamped my feet to keep warm but it was hard not to say a word at Nick who stood about looking at his kit with an air of lassitude. The sun sent a wave of low light across the basin and for a minute the snow about us gleamed sandy-coloured before a cloud edge drew in from the west and smudged the hilltops. The sun went and the light grew sullen.

Our movements promised to be as slow as yesterday's. We might have saved time by crossing the frozen Gorm Loch Mor but I didn't trust the ice, and instead we traced its winding shoreline and bore west on rising ground. Boulders at random littered the terrain, some of the erratics providing a home for dwarf and wind-harassed trees, together with the growth on those islets of the lochs the last relics of an ecologically richer past.

Although we wanted to reach a saddle known as Bealaich a'Mhadaidh our way was impeded by a large burn. Partially frozen, it dropped over small falls and bristled even after a week of frost. Only by going around the loch in the corrie above could we avoid it, but that would add an hour and probably more to the day, an hour we didn't have. It was impossible to cross at this point so we ploughed up, following its bank, I breaking trail until the burn narrowed to just a few yards. Ice extended from both banks but water rushed between boulders in the main channel. We stripped to bare legs, Nick protecting his feet with plastic crocs, I using an old pair of insoles and over these I pulled some thin socks. I stepped in. Almost immediately the ice collapsed and I was in up to my thighs. It was safer to smash the ice with each heel and wade. I shouted as I reached the far bank and turned to watch Nick. He went in a little upstream where the ice looked more solid but it gave way just the same and it was his turn to yell and when he reached me blood was running from a cut on his leg and melting the snow.

The first breath of clement air reached us as we pushed up a shoulder, the snow here at its thinnest, and though we climbed steeply it felt the best going for days, certainly easier than in any part of the basin. From our position we could see the frozen lochs and how the ice was crossed with abstract bands, signatures of freeze-thaw cycles prevalent in the fortnight prior. Away from the lochs and in the snowfields of Corie a'Mhadhaidh was a litter of boulders, angular pieces that from this distance seemed like pebbles broadcast by a hand of a giant. As if they might sprout into something. Ben Klibreck over in the east was still in sun and we could see Ben Armine and Creag Mhor anchored on the edge of Sutherland and in far places the dark forms of conifers against the snow, pictographs and symbols from a pagan past.

Loch nan Cuaran at the col was under deep drifts which we reached at dusk. The solitary hills of Sutherland were largely swamped by cloud and only in one narrow window was there a wavering orb of light on some distant cliff face. The temperature had risen to above freezing and when Nick caught me up he said he was relieved we were out of the basin, though not from a fear of being trapped.

Far below the river sank into its limestone valley and the hamlet of Inchnadamph there in its crook. I could remove my mittens on our descent and shed my outer shell as the air noticeably warmed. We found the path and on it were today's bootprints, they leading to a darkening and snowless valley, houselights appearing and electric beams from the odd car moving north and south, white points coming together and red receding tail-lights. Congealed ice made a hazard of the path and this continued below the snowline and almost to the first house, the windows curtained against the night save at one the silhouette of a figure, its back to us or watching, but no one outside did we see, no cars in the visitors' carpark and no noise of anything as we crossed the road.

Running wide and deep in the glen the River Loanan was the day's last barrier. I knew it would soon be in spate and so impassable, indeed it might be already. At the head of Loch Assynt we found the river still sluggish but at this point far too deep so went upstream, testing its depth at two or three places until a section where it was almost still. Stripped of our lower garments and boots tied to the crown of our sacs we went in over our waists, though compared to the ice bath earlier it felt almost balmy. Away from the bank we pitched on rough pasture by a small burn. I tethered my many guylines to rocks for security lest nightwinds pour down from the heights. Nick didn't bother. In any case he only had two guys, he said.

Three

My sleep was broken by rain and the pitch of a rising burn and with no let-up I went outside with my torch. The burn had more than doubled in size. It boiled half white and its noise mastered even that of the wind that rushed in from the south. I tightened some of the guys and looked over at Nick's tent. With each punch it stove inwards and I found it hard to believe anyone could be asleep in there. I fiddled with a loose strap on my head-torch and managed to cut my beam. A sudden and complete blackness. I stood unsteady with my back to the weather but even after a minute could make out neither sky nor land or even a hand passed before me.

In the grey light of dawn the land presented a hammered look. Banks of cloud crossing the mountains and much of yesterday's snow reduced to torrents that slashed the hillslopes. Yesterday's river swept past brimful and urgent. Having veered north in the small hours the wind now came gusting in across the loch and as I breakfasted another squall clattered the tent with rain and hail.

We divvied out the contents of the cache and these extra items gave Nick an added conundrum when the time came to pack. Supplies for four days, five at a stretch, enough I hoped to see us to the lands of Strath Mulzie in the south.

Loch Assynt is one the great unspoilt lochs of the west, six miles from head to mouth, the largest body of fresh water in a district with an abundance of water. A road runs along its northern shore, the bitumen foreshadowed by thousands of years of usage as a route from the interior to coastal homesteads. Another route used to trace the south side, a cart track serving the sheilings and summer pastures, and there's rumour this was once the main thoroughfare to the west. Marked on early hand-drawn maps, now barely the faintest trace of it remains. Nature reclaiming its own and a good thing, the ruined sheilings and rough fields as well. Today the land is steep and broken and some of it wrapped in tunics of old woodland, last of these parts and some of the last in Scotland.

The hanging woods of An Coimhleum extend almost to the head of the loch but they gather in density on the north slope of a great spur, and after more than a week of open hill there was a strange enclosed feeling as we slipped among the groves. Sheltered from man and beast the birch grew tall and with a rich understorey of rowan and holly. At the corner of the spur the land steepened into buttes and great fallen boulders and we went along by ledges and gaps, hands around an erratic, picking over a slope of rubble so thick with growths it had virtually disappeared. Trees bent skywards from every starting angle, trees thriving in the thinnest of soils, their roots teasing apart crannies and faults or splayed over a rockface like the spiny legs of giant arachnids. Everywhere water seeped and dripped and only in the recesses of overhangs by colonies of ferns were there dry and dark places for denizens of the wood or even vacant lots abandoned long ago by creatures that once prevailed here.

Leaving the spur the angle lessened and the ground was now a mattress of bell heather and blueberry without leaf. On the trees emerging from this carpet were all manner of mosses and lichen, pale green, sage and ash by colour. Trunks bowed from the earth and you could not see their bark so covered were they. I noticed an antique holly whose living trunk ran along the ground like a ship's rope, its glossy foliage without thorns and I thought that spoke much about where it grew. In the densest part of the wood where limbs embraced in a kind of wattle and the captured air was almost still we came upon a small clearing, a near level place on this north slope with the canopy arching over like sheltering arms and a surround of knotty stumps like some secret place from a child's storybook, and I thought if I rested here and didn't move would I ever be found? Would I want to be?

The old wood with its tilting boulders and tall heather made for a snail's progress, which was about right as there was no familiar line, no sign of people, not their spoor and nothing of paths. This changed as the trees ranged more sparsely and we followed a narrow and descending alley made by the cloven-footed beasts, the rain against us now and clouds low and loch beginning to smoke.

From here we chose to trace each headland as they appeared. It gave our route a circuitous feel but we saw also its vagaries, and while going higher might perhaps have involved a shorter distance it was rarely so in time.

Even by the lochside were pockets of thawing snow and some of the ground still hard with frost. Groups of Caledonian pine planted a while ago began to appear, but the land was now largely open and crossing it we kept high above Rubhna na Moine and dropped through thinning birch and stepped over a burn to a narrow strip of beach. A reddish shingle here banked up by various high waters, jetsam on the heather and tree roots weathered into stanchions. The sky darkened. Mist screened the far shore. We turned against the weather and stood like tailor's dummies, unmoving, mute, hoods up as hail blew past and peppered the water like showers of rice. We thought to let it pass but the damp and cold had us shaking and we set off again soon enough.

Where unfenced the land appeared run over by deer and their trails commonly ran through the scattered wood, the trees here mostly old and some torn down by gales which further opened up the hillside, and so year by year the trees were toppled. In such weather the deer seek shelter among the remaining groves and browse away on the few saplings and in doing so deny themselves a future sanctuary.

When I studied the sky between cloudbursts I thought dusk would soon be upon us. Nick was naturally cautious when walking in such terrain and I probably should have allowed for this but more likely we had stopped too often and been just too beguiled. In any case time was a notion solely of our heads. Each afternoon I looked for the sun on its course, and if not seen, which was usual, then the calibration of light as it notched down, our days already following a pattern. We were never so late to break camp that forenoon didn't usually have an hour or two to run and that meant seven hours to journey before dark and seven hours was not enough. I could sense the approach of twilight anyway or maybe I'd just slipped into prior ways and read auguries attuned from years in the hills. The dark came anyway and as the days passed I began to call it down, not because it marked cessation and promise of rest, for it usually didn't, but rather I found a truth there. Our hours of small progress nothing to the blind wheeling earth and rising planets and stars and nether regions of the void and beauty past reckoning.

The dark was coming early and at one of the many burns we stopped to heat water for tea. I knew there was not much more than a mile to our reckoned camp by a ruin still known locally as Tubeg and marked as such. Around a last promontory we looked west to the curve of a bay, the land now almost a silhouette and without feature and the water at its side softly rippling.

We paced the bank of a deep and foaming burn. I went off on a running jump that got me to a rock in the middle, a step to another and a step to the far side. But I missed and went in and filled both boots with icy water. Our headtorches on, we searched for referents and bent inland to Loch a'Mhuilinn, rounding its sodden fringe to another burn, this one tree-lined. Another jump and I went in again. I climbed out and waited. Dark had come so quickly I feared clouds had banked and would deliver another drenching. Nick's piecemeal beam reached me through the branches. When close enough I offered advice and gestured with my torch. He jumped and got as wet as I had. Clumps of gorse skylighted the slope ahead and there we found the ruin of Tubeg and beside it another, the insides all rubble but at its front cropped grass ran to a shallow depression, this fended on three sides by dense gorse shrubbery. Man and beast had long been using this place for refuge, especially on such nights.

Putting the tent up was delayed as hail duly came, sweeping unhindered the miles of loch, and found us with our backs to the sheltering outside wall and each of us either side of where the front door once hung. Hail and rain blew through the gap there and across our beams and hardly relented as we fixed our tents and made taut each guy. I made an untidy pile of my wet things and sunk into my bag and cooked tinned fish and vegetables and pasta for us both and called Nick when ready who came barefoot over the fallen ice like a penguin to collect his share. I'd done the cooking, he could do the walking. Squalls rolled in at intervals and the wind through the ruin was like a thing demented. It sieved the gorse and played in pockets and the general rush of it over the hills a constant. I listened and lay warm with a brew and reckoned no manufactured comfort could surpass this, the cradling heat in my hands and not having to move beyond a turn or roll for the entire night. At least I hoped I wouldn't.

Lightning briefly lit the shifting tent walls and in the ensuing and sudden dark, thunder clanged over land and loch. Hail rattled as never before. I shouted to Nick and he back but barely a word fathomable and only later when it quieted could we talk. I said I'd heard of hail shredding tents in other countries. Nick said it had happened in Canada when he lived there but as far as he knew never in this country so we needn't worry. We spoke of the walk. Nick said the hard miles were good, especially those when there was much for the eye, for they were a huge distraction from his day to day concerns and he agreed the woods were a thing of beauty. How could anyone not see that? But he also said he needed to rest soon, a whole day when he would not be required to move.

The storm passed and by morning the air felt drier if just as raw. Some new snow marked out the sandstone tiers of Quinag across the loch and its burns still tumbled white, the land there having a tired and worn look, treeless and without even much ling, just grass and spiked rush and a sour green over it all.

I poked about the shielings waiting for Nick. I'd heard the house here was occupied until the 1950s. An old rowan sprouting from one of its walls had many years before been sawn and now grew as a pollard with many spurs. The surrounding gorse rocked in the wind. January still had a week to run yet the uppermost buds were trying to open. I picked one to smell and thought of spring but it was a false sign. The coastal fringe here had its own climate and was nothing to the wild high country where we were headed.

The map showed a path but there wasn't one, a line through heather and no more than where deer and sheep had trampled. Anyway we should have stuck to the shore as our perceived shortcut was not that and we strayed too far south. Rather than cross the burn we followed it up and found ourselves lost in a deep groove with views of the loch gone. So steeply-sided we needed our hands to climb out. We dropped down the hill and found a vague path skirting a forestry fence, all of which took an hour or more. The high fence demarcated and protected nearly a square mile of restored native woodland, and once established the knolls and slopes of this headland will again be a haven for all. The restoration is part of a grand vision of the paper owners of this 44,000-acre estate, the Assynt Foundation, whose purchase of the land in 2005 was one of the first under the provisions of the Scottish Land Reform Act (2003). Their long-term vision is to restore natural woodland cover to some fifty percent of the land area, a temperate rainforest from Ledmore Junction to Loch Assynt and in time surrounding the hills of Suilven, Canisp, Cul Mor and Cul Beag. The Foundation seeks a connection with the land that was once commonplace but now is echoed only in the scattered ruins and placenames on the map. Bealach Aird na Seilge is 'pass of the height of the hunting', Loch a'Mhuilium, 'loch of the mill', Doire Daimh, 'wood of the ox'.

It was odd that my map had no mention of the lochan we passed and I thought it seasonal only, just an overspill of all the rains of late. I guessed the path was part of the old route on the south side, for centuries cattle driven here to the summer pastures. The way had vegetated over from underuse but its mark was still there and it went contouring like a clever road and gathered in easy switchbacks to the bealach and thence to the loch's egress and River Inver.

The afternoon seemed to vanish as we swung inland again and south to the hills. The Allt an Tiaghaich we now crossed drained many sizeable hill lochs and unvisited corries on the north slopes of Canisp. The stepping stones were submerged and we waded knee-deep the freezing waters and in the grey light of late afternoon climbed west to the pass. Suilven sprung into the frame, snow along its sandstone bands and clouds streamed from the summit of Caisteal Liath, a magnificent hill even in the gloom of a short winter's day. For minutes we watched the play of cloud then dropped to a chain of small lochs that retained the last of the day's brightness, against it the dark isles were globs of land adrift and their trees fernlike in outline. We walked into dark and never did use our torches. I was ahead and stopped thrice to listen for Nick's coming. So quiet and hardly a breath of wind on the loch. Rustle of boots over heather, sound of steady breathing, a dark moving shape. The trail crossed a connecting burn between two lochs and the stepping stones here conspicuous by the sluice of water in their channels and at the last we crept by feel alone to a dark and empty bothy.

Even four thick walls couldn't insulate us from the sound of storm that blew in sometime during the night. Rain in salvoes on the zinc roof, a forerunner of wind from Glencanisp cleaving the bothy and coming down the flue with a pneumatic hiss and a constant drumming. It worried my dreams and woke me. I'd dreamt of being trapped by rising waters, my strength ebbing as I attempted to wade, then swim, weightless and past all hope. I sat up in the dark. Drips from a leaking gutter, the wind pitching around the chimney stack. A mouse tiptoeing on the stone floor. Thereafter I dozed fitfully. Even in the grey light I could see Suilven had been largely stripped of snow but if it was milder it didn't feel so. Nick slept through my scrapings and rattles which accompanied breakfast. We wouldn't be going anywhere in any case. I'd promised Nick a rest. No day had been easy and by now his feet were a little sore, swollen even. The bothy's location and the timing of our arrival seemed propitious enough. I didn't believe our tents would have survived if we'd stayed in the open. That was confirmed when, outside collecting water, I was spun sideways by a gust and only by hopping like a crow did I manage to stay upright.

When I got back Nick was half out of his sleeping bag making porridge. Some raisins and a spoon of coconut powder on the steaming gruel, a combination he swore by.

'Well,' he said, taking a mouthful, 'I wouldn't have fancied your tent in this wind.'

'It would have been tested for sure.'

'Tested and trashed.'

'Just as well we're here then. What a haven this place is.'

'Certainly is. Listen to that.' The wind rose and we both looked roofwards. The joists creaked and a cobweb in the corner wobbled. 'We could easily have been caught out. It was dark and late. What then?'

'In which case we make camp and brace ourselves for the worst. We both have bivies.'

Holding a mug of tea I peered through the window. The grey castle of Suilven, Caisteal Liath, was half-hidden in fast-moving cloud. As I looked this seemed to have a hole punched through it and for a few seconds I saw the entire dome of the hill.

'It's the sudden gusts that do it,' I said. 'The rogue winds. Lying in a tent you can hear the big ones coming and your last chance is to grab the centre pole and hold on. But you can't do that all night. When the knock-out comes you have to be ready. I was caught out in the Cairngorms and another time on Skye. Both times a pole snapped and the outer ripped. I was on my own and a long way from the road.'

'What happened?'

'I dived into my bivy. On Skye I got under a boulder, some old den for animals I reckoned. You don't go anywhere in winter without a bivouac sac. It's a lifeline.'

Nick thought on this while spooning his porridge.

'But that's nothing to a friend camped one night on the slopes of Foinaven,' I said. 'This guy doesn't embellish and I believe his story, the kind of guy that disappears into the hills for weeks at a time and usually it's hard to get him to say anything, but he did tell me this.'

'Foinaven?'

'Yeah, that hill we saw to the north when we crossed over into Assynt, remember? He was camped high in a storm and was already half in his bivy and hanging onto his main supporting pole when he heard a massive roar come from above, like one of those low-flying jets. Next second he was airborne, literally off the ground. He remembers nothing save waking to a mess of nylon and broken and bent poles, open sky above. He bundled everything up and hobbled down the hill and flagged the first car. The driver was appalled. "You seen the state of your face?" he said. All bloodied and bruised. He was taken straight to Raigmore in Inverness.'

'How strong a wind was that? A hundred?'

'Probably more. When you consider gusts of a hundred and seventy have been recorded here you wonder what goes unrecorded, especially when you realise there's only a handful of hills in Scotland where measuring takes place. That storm earlier this month hardly raised an eyebrow in the media yet it was the biggest blow for years. Not many folks live up here so it's hardly news. And it conveniently bypassed the Central Belt, but it was some wind. We saw the wires and trees down. Being caught in it that would have been interesting.'

'Don't doubt it,' Nick said.

'Maybe that's what happened to Clive.'

'How d'you mean?'

'Of course we don't know much of the detail, but the day he went missing was a day of storm. A Sunday in late March. The last big blow of the winter. From the southeast as well, a dry one. They're legendary in the Highlands, and probably the most feared. A helm wind they call it in some places, my sailing dad told me about that.'

'Helm wind? Not heard of that.'

'Up here virtually everything comes from the southwest or west. Folk are used to dealing with them. But a sou'easter in spring hits your underbelly and this one came all the way from Siberia. I was home over the weekend and just walking the dog was an expedition. The windchill was shocking. I had no idea Clive was out, let alone where he'd gone.'

Nick pursed his lips. 'On the Monday I got your text saying he'd not turned up for work.'

'My phone was red. The police were in touch around mid-day. Family and friends started calling. Had he been out with me? Surely I knew something? Truth was I didn't. I'd got a message from him on Thursday, about a football game I think. But nothing on his plans for the weekend. The forecast was terrible. Everyone knew this thing was coming.'

Nick had stopped eating.

'Did you think he was alive?'

'In my heart I hoped he was of course, but my head said something else. I had a strong feeling that whatever happened to Clive the wind had played a big part.'

Nick scraped out the last of his porridge and looked across the room to the rain-smeared window and then looked at the empty fireplace. Nothing in the way of fuel to burn and neither of us inclined to walk the miles to gather any, so we lay wrapped against the cold and read and talked the hours away. Nick speculated on matters evolutionary, whether human intelligence was finite or even regressive which at least would explain the rise of tribal politics and our failure to deal with climate change. He also wondered if some soul would brave the inclement weather and visit the old sheiling. I thought the first likely, the second not so. I said human nature and human greed are two sides of the same coin. The mindset we've inherited since the Enlightenment, of economic growth and material advancement at any cost has created the present environmental crisis, the greatest threat facing us. This can't go on, yet our reaction has been Palaeolithic. That's fear talking, I said, nations staking claims and squabbling over scarce resources like empires of old, only this time we all lose.

As to visitors, if these conditions were foretold why would anyone be foolish enough to venture into them?

Given the thaw I was surprised how cold it was, cold enough to keep us well-wrapped. Nick was lying on the bench bunk in his sleeping bag, headphones firmly over his ears and eyes closed so I couldn't tell if he was in fact awake. I put my book down and thought of Clive choosing to go out in that weather.

I remembered him at Sandwood Bay up on the north coast of Sutherland. A wild day with stinging sand and crashing waves. We'd rock-hopped the burn draining Sandwood Loch and traced the rocky margins of the beach to the small headland. Beyond this was another sandy bay, easy to reach at low tide but at that time water surrounded the rocks. Come on, he said, let's do it, the water's not deep, and he was off, wading and shouting. I followed. A high wave came in and nearly carried us away, its backwash like a rope pulling around my waist. Our boots were soaked, our trousers were soaked, but we got clear of the water and padded about on the sand, Clive was ecstatic and laughing.

No one did arrive but just before turning in the waxing moon rose above Suilven, so clear there was earthshine in its shadow. Cloud came in and it was seen no more.

Four

By torchlight we breakfasted and packed and were early onto the old floorboards of Assynt and on a path scoured from ancient bedrock to face the first sun in days, a sparkle in the burns and on crystal outcroppings of gneiss and red gouts of moss in the weave of the moor, the detail going to general umber as we climbed to a broader view. I stopped and waited by a burn brimful with yesterday's rain, it running white and divided by rock piping that seemed the stone fingers of a hand holding up the flow. Suilven's high terracing and rock sleeves were all gridlined in fresh snow and a little further on we came to Loch Gainimh, a mile of dark water and here the west wind blustery and raw. With the sun gone the loch lent a sense of enclosure, steep slopes crowding it and blocking the paltry January light and I was glad to be climbing again, skirting Canisp that rose so abruptly we only saw it properly hours later on the plain to the south. Suilven ran through its repertoire of guises. The tiered battlements on its long side began to compress as we moved east then south, and slowly there appeared a great furrowed nose, an enormous head lying on its back facing the heavens.

It was gone soon enough. Dark banks of cloud rolling in and smothering the hills behind and we watched their progress while lunching by a frozen and nameless loch. We finished our scalding brews and were back on the path and hooded up and approaching the highest point when the squall hit. Hail and snow so thick we could hardly see the way. The force of it troubling. In five minutes the ground had whitened and the gusts were such we were forced to stop and crouch and wait its passing, at least until sure of our footing.

The path become sandstone pavement of random patterns like crazy tiling, then we marched over conglomerate and after that quartz blocks, some filmed in slime, so we went about gingerly, especially in the wind. The path sank to the ancient trench of Cam Loch and in between showers emerged the northern cliffs of Cul Mor ribboned in snow, then hills of sandstone that footed higher ranges to the south, none of whose crowns were visible. The loch gave no shelter as another squall came in to bundle us to the Ullapool road. Cars heard and seen in the distance but none passed as we crossed the river by the bridge, the waters today deep and impassable.

On a greying afternoon we traced the west bank as the river went over a series of falls and rapids, and from its gorge-like banks there grew a profusion of woodland, birch bent skywards and grey limbs of willows and bony rowans. Above the falls floodwater covered the banks and pushed us out on a detour until we reached Loch Urigill, the surface here placid, as if by crossing parishes we'd crossed climate zones as well. The old Foreland of Assynt now behind us and we were back among the chaos of the Moine rocks. No path by the shore but the sward green and calcareous and much grazed and easy on our feet and in places breached by pale exposures of limestone, great boulders deeply fissured by the sometime action of water and growing among them tormented birch through which a light wind seethed.

In the fading day I waited at such a place for Nick and perused the map for a spot to camp. A ruin to the south, two miles away, three at most. Nick's feet were sore again but he said he could do the distance no problem. The old place was sited by a river that flowed into Urigill so we shore-walked and reached the flatlands by its mouth and with our lights began to follow the river's meandering course upwards. Although gentle going, the way seemed more miles than the map could capture, the river chuckling or running deep but always another bend or loop or over some alluvial bank or piled gravel. When expecting our beams to find the grey dyking of an enclosure there was just another wash, the mercurial sheen of water as it braided and ran muttering among isles of stones and sluiced small channels. Occasionally we abandoned the bank in a little sortie, thinking that perhaps the house had been built at some remove from a river liable to flood. But it just went on and another hour passed and I wondered at our effort just to find this place and to lie by it for the night. Perhaps it bespoke a desire to be where other folk have lived. Not since the north coast ten days ago had we seen or spoken to another human. The ruin promised only a sheltering wall for our tents yet the knowledge folk had stayed here with their families was an ounce of comfort in an empty land.

Our torch-beams swung over two tumbled shells, their outer walls softened these years by lichen and mosses, their guts piled with rubble. One house nearly down and the other still with a dozen timbers reaching skywards and holding the last memory of a roof.

Nick released his sac from his shoulder and sat on the grass, leaning with his back against a wall. He looked shattered. I ran my light along the planks. They rot and fall with passing seasons and in time only a heap of stones and a line in a census will tell of the lives here. Maybe the oldest person in the parish still living knew them but memories go and people don't ask, certainly not the young. I once met an old man fishing a small remote loch who said he'd been born in the wreckage of a nearby croft. He said no more save when it had been abandoned and save what fish might bite and I left him to climb a hill and when I returned he was gone. Now I wish I'd heard his story so I in turn could have passed it on. Folk memory is unreliable but it only takes a link to be broken for the knowledge to disappear. Our ruins and monuments going back thousands of years are silent for that reason.

I wondered when these buildings were forsaken as homes and why, and for how many years after had they given wayfarers and hill tramps crude sanctuary. No sign of recent fires despite old rafters and joists strewn about, some half concealed by moss and turf in the ground around as if at one time the houses were ransacked.

In the dark and in such a state I didn't dare put a foot inside. There was no space by the walls so we pitched on short grass just downwind and crawled into our shelters beneath a crescent moon and a few early stars. Later it began to rain and a cold wind sprang up to ferret about my vestibule and play havoc with my stove. What remained of the evening was all rain and for a long time I just lay there and revelled in the noise of it.

It never really let up and the elements conspired for much of the night to rob me of sleep. When still dark I threw Nick a call. I spread the map as best as I could and gauged the day's travel. All wild country to the south and little by way of paths. I was so slow in getting ready that when I emerged in the wet to unpeg the fly Nick was already up, clad in waterproofs and crouching and studying the ground where a few pieces of gear lay. He was in the last throes of packing. He looked over. I was cramming stuff into my sac.

'What's the hurry?' he said and grinned to himself. We said little. A wet prospect, a load of walking over high hills.

Through a hole in the mist was a rain-drenched view over Assynt, the higher tops in fresh snow and old wreaths tailing into cloud like toothed parts of vanished beasts. Loch Urigill was half seen then not at all as we climbed into cloud and navigated by holding to the river, knowing the moor to be riddled with ditches. By this way we came to a hidden ravine, both sides carrying a tapestry of vegetation, birch, rowan, willow, last season's fernery, the misty light giving the greens and browns a luminous quality and I thought I'd never seen such richness. For a couple of miles at least we traced every bend, every straight, knowing more or less we were heading south to the watershed and as the rain eased to drizzle the river opened and climbed more gently, losing its width and bustle. There were many feeder streams and alluvial banks of clean pasture or spikes of rush and a last harried tree before the open moor, pitted and eroded and crevassed in long trenches that ran like crazy guttering, each to be crossed and all floored in mud or thawing snow.

From the bealach we dropped to a near-ruinous structure at the upper reaches of Strath nan Lon and in its dubious shelter boiled water for our lunchtime drinks. Old dykes enclosed the place and I guessed it once functioned as a sheep station and this building a shelter for herders. One part still retained a crude metal roof and we stood under this supping our brews. On the ground plastic bags and rusting coils of wire and rotting timbers and in one corner the severed hind leg of a deer that had been placed just so like some offering. Through windowless gaps a damp wind came in and stole about the interior. The lintel stone over the entrance seemed ready to collapse. Just the slightest nudge. We tiptoed out.

In such trackless country we soon came to a series of narrow lochs in seasonal flood, the surface troubled and holding grey ragged clouds and heathers and dull greens of peripheral hills. Maybe in spring its waters would teem with the play of waders and divers but today it was hard to imagine a more lonesome spot, silent save the wind. The last loch held a number of strange tear-shaped isles and from its shores we drifted east by a burn, the land falling now as we reached Rappach Water, one of the infant rivers of the Oykel which drains all the hills of this largely forgotten corner. At a bend in the river I paused at a house half gone in ruin. The building marooned in a shallow moat that lapped at its foundations. One of the gables presented a severe and irreversible tilt and among the rubble was the iron fretwork of a bed or cot.

When Nick caught up he said his feet ached. I showed him the map and we continued along the river and counted the burns east, a path now of sorts, the Rappach growing in commotion and falling by ramps and rapids. Ashen-coloured rocks alongside it layered and slanted. Close to another ruin the waters divided around an island topped with rank heather and a single antique tree and gave a throaty echo as they swept beneath a low cliff. The second ruin was much older and more gone in decay, its walls so broken and reduced by passing winters they would soon be just footings in the sward, a nuisance to the wind and in time not even that.

Nick's movement was laboured. Each of my waits a little longer and on this clouded afternoon the day was already closing. In the half-light the path's line grew weak. By the edge of a wood on the opposite bank of the Rappach and some four miles from here lay a cache of food we needed to reach if we were to eat tonight. The path we were on led to the only footbridge over the river. Miss that and we would have to wade.

For as long as possible we held off using our lights, thinking we could trace the pale wet gleam against the dark moor, but we couldn't and despite searching high and low never saw it again. The path had gone.

I told Nick it didn't matter and reckoned it only a mile to the bridge. Let's keep a high line, I said, but somehow as the banks steepened and the river-noise grew we were drawn down and got snared in a hanging wood. A tricky route through pale and bent trees, each knotted specimen seeming to occupy the one safe footing and to pass we had to hook an arm around some branch and duck and swing like startled apes. One slip would put us in the river. Nick was never far behind, sometimes his light bobbing like a marker buoy or it appeared to flash a message through a matrix of trunks and branches. In return I would point an answering light in his direction and run my hand over it. Then I remembered something and stopped. I shouted his name instead.

I'd been counting steps, five hundred, a thousand, five hundred more, a mile by my thinking and at this point ran my beam over the water, downstream as far as it would reach. Nothing but the sheen of water so we forged on into a night, giving no quarter to fatigue and no thought to it, driven not by hunger but simply by the fact of being driven. Time spiralled and the evening was far gone when I parried through some trees and stepped onto a beaten path and in a minute found the narrow suspension bridge. The whole structure swayed when I stepped onto it, the dark waters racing beneath. A building on the far side that once served as a rudimentary schoolhouse was now a kind of bothy, pretty spartan with a couple of simple rooms and no fireplace. The air was thick with damp when we entered and just standing there chilled us to the bone. Our cache lay hidden a quarter of a mile down the track and with empty packs we fairly bounced along and dropped into the woods and on hands and knees pawed around a fallen log like hungry bears. Supplies aplenty for a feast tonight whilst the remainder would see us over the mountains to Glascarnoch and the Fannichs, or so we hoped.

After our meal I was ready for sleep. Nick had just come in from a last visit outside. He stamped his boots on the boards.

'The snow's coming,' he said.

'In that case it's good we made it here, well worth dragging our feet the last few miles to avoid a night out.'

'Reckon I was doing most of the dragging. I was getting a little confused with your light. It kept going out. Why was that? Your battery?'

'No, I kept my hand over it, or I just switched it off when waiting.'

'Why?'

'I didn't think you would appreciate it, I mean you have a thing about being watched, or rather the knowledge you're being watched.'

'True, I do, but not tonight. I needed to know where you were.'

'You once misread my light.'

'What – this evening?'

'No, way back.'

Nick was lighting his stove for a brew. A hiss from the flame. He looked up.

'You threatened me with a branch,' I said.

'The An Teallach trip?'

'That's the one.'

Nick laughed.

'It wasn't funny at the time.'

'Don't remember much about it. I was too far gone. Delirious even. My account is the one you've fed me over years and I've no reason to doubt you. It's your tale.'

'All true,' I said.

That was more than ten years ago. In the aftermath Nick had not wanted to talk of the matter and I didn't ask, but in time and in the quiet of some bothy he would sometimes mention it. He said he didn't remember much save small details, snatches of conversation, the wavering lights. As if by talking he could give it a shape and file it away. In the frigid air our breaths condensed and we spoke of it again.

I'd vaguely heard of marshlights, strange flickering lights that hang over bogs and are said to be born of methane. Old stories mention the lights receding if approached and drawing travellers from safe paths. In my years of wandering I'd never witnessed such phenomena nor knew anyone who claimed to have. Until that day with Nick.

Sultry and warm for autumn, we'd come over the hills from Little Loch Broom and set up camp by a ruin in Strath na Sealga. The midges were so bad that after dumping our tents we headed south for a remote group of hills and slept soundly under a draughty rock at twenty-five hundred feet. Two of our party of five were new to such rough hill travel but embraced the adventure. Nick had plenty of pedigree but was out of shape and struggled, not so much on the ascents but on the loose sandstone and quartz coming down. He was painfully slow and it was late when everyone gathered on the day's last hill, Beinn a' Chlaidheimh. A decision was made to split the party, three going ahead while I stayed with Nick. He sat against the cairn breathing heavily. He confessed he was near his limit and wasn't sure if he could reach camp. We were two hours coming down and darkness overtook us long before we crossed the gleam of water in Strath na Sealga. We fumbled along with no torches, gauging land-marks by their vague shapes and the rough path by the feel of it. I'd chivvied Nick constantly during the descent but he'd now reached the end, at least in his head, and any encouragement was answered by mumblings and outbursts. The last mile was punctuated by halts, each longer than the last. Perhaps a couple of hundred yards from camp Nick stopped again and sat down. I said I would go on and get a brew ready. I left Nick slumped in the heather. It was near midnight and quiet at the ruin, the others in their sleeping bags, someone snoring. I boiled water and waited, expecting Nick in few minutes. I went outside with my friend's headtorch and flashed it again and again. I thought about yelling his name but rather than wake the others I retraced my steps and gained the point where I'd left Nick. He'd vanished. I ran my light over the shallow river and along the bank. Nick was half crouching by a shrubby willow, a few yards away. Holding a large branch over his head. His voice boomed. 'YOOOU. Turn off that light. Come any closer and I'll crack you one!' I froze and yelled, 'Nick, it's me, a friend, your friend!' Then as if coming out of some trance he broke into laughter. He laughed and laughed. He said he'd seen lights. Of course he seen a light, I said, my light. No, he said. Lights. More than one. He'd studied them. At first they'd mysteriously come and go but then began to approach, as if he was being hunted. He'd gone to ground and felt about for some cudgel and waited.

Nick held his steaming mug in both palms and touched it to his lips.

'Your light gave me a right scare,' he said. 'I do remember that.'

'Genuine fear on this side as well. That was a big branch.'

Later I lay in my sleeping bag reading with gloved hands but more I wondered whether you can truly know someone even after years of shared experiences. Clive loved the story. It tickled him that I might have been clobbered, mistaken for some lantern-carrying leprechaun out there on the moor. He never tired of hearing it. I smiled. A great shadow of my book on the far wall. Turning a page slowly as if from a huge ledger. A pulse of wind over the roof and tap-tap of snow on the windowpane. When the school closed the building was used by the estate as a storeroom, the door usually unlocked and you could shelter from the rain among rolls of fencing wire, bales of hay, bags of animal feed. In those days you tested your vehicle's suspension on the potholed track and drove here. Now a gate prevents such easy access.

There were other times. One afternoon pausing here for a break the day before Hogmanay. More than a foot of snow on the ground and our car stuck in a drift some way down the track. With all that wine Clive's rucksac had an oddly mis-shapen look. Additional bottles in carrier bags and one in his coat pocket and he clinked with each step like a ragman vendor going croft to croft. At the foot of Seana Bhraigh seven miles to the south was an old byre, one of the hardest to reach bothies in Scotland, especially when the approaches were under snow. We only got there the following day, the blanket of snow leaving us so drained the Old Year slipped by unmarked and with us asleep and sober on moth-eaten mattresses. The walls of the byre gave out their cold but next day we collected enough fuel to fire away the dampness and drank and sung and later toasted the rising moon, the frozen hills like drapes from a great starched tablecloth. I closed my eyes at the memory.

Hail periodically rattled the metal roof and by first light I could see a little snow on the window-ledges. Nick didn't answer my call. He'd been up briefly but I'd not heard a sound from him since. Outside cloud was low and new snow covered the land. A bitter wind tailed down the valley. I went back in and straight into my bag. We weren't moving today at any rate. Nick's swollen feet had forced a rest and lying there I tried to think about what this meant. His feet might harden as we moved south, or they would get worse. Either way they needed care if we were ever going to reach Knoydart.

Nick occupied the west room with the bench bunk and when later I knocked and got no response I opened the door a crack. The flysheet of his tent was draped across the window blocking the light and in the dimness I made out a muffled recumbent figure, his chest falling and rising and small puffs of vapour condensing above him like a bad miasma. He finally showed around noon. I brewed soup as he paced about, balling his fists against the cold. He said he'd been fatigued in the build-up to the trip and not in the least ready for such a travail. I said, you can walk yourself into shape. It wasn't just about fitness, he said. The months before hadn't been easy. Not something he could really explain though its shadow had so burdened him that during the first week in the wild he said it was like living under a cloak that blocked out the light. Since then, well, the walking's been tough, very tough, and his feet at times have been giving him hell but despite all that he was rediscovering something, a thing he'd almost forgotten, the rhythm of a long walk, the beauty of moving, brief moments of joy even. He said he hoped sincerely the walk would aid his recovery. So yes, the walking was a kind of therapy. And he was also doing it for Clive.

All day the outside pressed against the schoolhouse, pinging hailstones, the fitful wind. I asked Nick about the Hogmanay trip with Clive. Yes, he remembers it well. A time when life was generally good and he was holding down a teaching job. Only two years before he'd discovered the Highlands and especially its winter aspect.

'This is my season,' he said, 'I love the cold and dark, the challenges. I love it because other people hate it. Does that make sense? That trip over New Year was one of the best. Staggering through those drifts, fronting that wind. It devours you completely, forces you to live entirely in the moment. To get through you have to call on something deep. Maybe that's it with me. That Hogmanay, yeah, I remember how we kept swapping the lead to break trail and even then were only getting a mile an hour, probably less. Clive even said he might have to shed some bottles.'

'Glad he didn't,' I said. 'Wine never tasted like that.'

'Especially when carted in by someone else.'

'Hey, I carried wine, but decanted it into something lighter. Clive just didn't care about the weight. It was Hogmanay. He wanted to party. Though even he couldn't drink everything.'

'What happened to the rest?'

'He buried them.'

'Don't remember that.'

'Nor could he. Don't bury stuff when you're hungover if you want to see it again is probably the message. Over the years he poked about with a shovel but we never found the wine. Probably still there.'

My pan began to purr and stream escaped into the frigid air. I rooted about for some teabags.

'Top-up?'

Nick nodded and grabbed his mug. I watched the water turn brown and tried the remember the taste of wine.

'I don't suppose we left a bottle in one of our parcels?' I said.

'We didn't. I don't touch that stuff, remember. I gave it up years ago. But it was a two-way traffic.'

'What do you mean?'

'Alcohol went out, sourdough came in.'

'Yeah, I remember. They called the Canadian pioneers "sourdoughs", so you're in good company.'

I tipped the tea into Nick's mug.

'It's funny,' I said, 'but after that trip I swore to Clive I'd get a pair of snowshoes.'

'What's funny about that?'

'Well, he didn't seem to know what to say. Probably thought I was little crazy. Or soft. You know, having all that kit. He only ever took the bare minimum. He usually had wet feet and I once asked him whether it was time he got himself some gaiters. He honestly didn't know what they were. I think he was forty before he bought himself waterproof overtrousers. His idea of camping was lying in a bivy bag with it open to the stars and if the rain came the rain came.'

'Yep, he was definitely hardcore.'

'I don't think he thought about it. Some folk have made their hardships into a way, a philosophy. You read about it in their blogs and reports and good luck to them. We've all gone a bit soft for sure, but Clive honestly seemed indifferent to most hardships. And he didn't care to tell you about it.'

'Did you?'

'Did I what?'

'Did you get those snowshoes?'

'Nah. Clive was right about kit. Who needs that stuff?'

Nick paced as we talked, a stocky hooded figure, hands deep in his pockets. I thought if you didn't know him he might have appeared vaguely intimidating. His broad frame built from years of channelling surplus energy into gym workouts. He knew his muscle-groups like a physio's wallchart. He pressed his nose against the small window.

'Can barely see a thing. It's wild.' Then he said his feet were better and refused my offer of painkillers. He was taking plenty pills as it was, he said.

The passing of a brief winter's day. Later I cooked up a meal and we ate it in our bags for it was too cold to do otherwise and I read the long evening through or lay in the flickering light with my thoughts, Nick snoring again, the last guttering candle, the wind about the roof and gable and thrash of it in the bare trees by the river.

Five

Our leaving the next day coincided with a 4x4 vehicle arriving in the snow and stopping. The window on the driver's side slid down. The local stalker. In the passenger seat was a young man and in the back a much older man. A protégé and client or maybe two clients. Both were wrapped in army fatigues. The stalker greeted us with a nod, we exchanged pleasantries and he asked where we'd come from, where we were bound. He listened and then suggested we might alter our route, for he and his party carried rifles and needed to take some hinds as part of the cull. I said in that case we would head further east, by the ruin of Upper Letters. The man nodded and seemed satisfied. He was about to go when I asked if he knew whether the bothy at Glenbeg was open, as we hoped to be there in two days if the weather held. The stalker thought for a moment. He claimed not to know of the bothy but said if it was anywhere near the glen of that name then it wasn't his patch. He said the man who holds title to those lands was bent on a regime of rewilding and who knows his views on bothies, their maintenance or otherwise. His window slid back up and the vehicle moved away.

For a mile or so we followed its ruts. Nick was visibly troubled by the change of schedule. He'd wanted an easy day for his feet but to placate the keeper we'd now have to climb into the hills and trace a high valley to a remote watershed. The snow-covered terrain promised every manner of obstacle. I was secretly pleased.

Putting aside sore feet, I thought the high route was in keeping, and anyway why reach a place by a beaten path in half a day when you could travel the hills and not get there even by nightfall?

Close to the deserted Corriemulzie Lodge we crossed a foot-bridge and set off up the snowy hillside as promised and were soon peering down at toy buildings and further up the track where the stalker's pick-up had halted and standing close by were darkly-clad figures with guns. They appeared to be gathered in conference. I thought they would have their business finished and be back for lunch as deer seemed plentiful. We saw in excess of a hundred before the day was done.

From our vantage the land had that routed look which even the snow couldn't soften. Treeless save for a few randomly planted strips of conifers where sheep and deer might congregate in a storm. In my years of coming here the only changes I ever saw were additional bulldozed tracks and new pools scooped out by a digger from the riverbed for the few salmon that make it beyond the falls, fewer by the year. We pulled around the shoulder and away from the main valley. Hills beckoned in the gauzy sunlight. Nick caught me up. He was enjoying himself again, he said, and glad to be away from the track and the hunters.

In a short while we'd contoured east and our eyes settled upon a shallow basin with its gently coiling burn. On its banks spikes of rush pushed through the snow and the water had a molten look. Something about it spoke to me and I remembered the last time I'd been this way. High summer a few years back. With Clive. Like today, we'd come by the tumbled shell of Upper Letters with the sound of larks and lapwings and descended to a small terrace by a pool and paused there to look for trout. Glare of water, flies dancing in sunshine. A brief moment but it came back true and real as if it had just been.

I pushed on and when I next spoke to Nick I had set up my stove on a boulder to melt snow. Ahead was a rising trackless land and I didn't think many folk came this way and over the years had never seen any. Beyond the watershed Seana Bhraigh and the pronged peak of Creag an Duine coalesced from shifting cloud, all monochrome, the latter with its shelving and ledges and strata storied up and tapering, as if to withstand the earth's shaking as once it probably did. Cloud closed in again and in the sullen light we focused more on where to place each step. Snow drifting a foot or more. It filled the ditches and our progress stalled, brisk where the wind had scoured, floundering in the banks. By following the burn we avoided the worse of the ditches but the burn petered out and with our lead gone we waymarked on Seana Bhraigh, now reduced to an outline in the mist as the day closed in.

Slowly the land began to tilt in our favour. We stopped to pick at old pine roots jutting through the snow and loaded our sacs and bore what sticks we could until so weighted our walking became little more than a shuffle. Gravity hauled us the last few hundred feet to loch and bothy. Snow had drifted against door and windows like a cottage in a child's picture-book. As usual we settled into the old byre, an attachment to the main and newly renovated bothy and for decades the only shelter for miles. Small and windowless but easier to heat than the main building and for me wrapped about with memories reaching back to a stormy

March day a quarter of a century before when I first took refuge here.

Of our gathered wood I set to work breaking and splitting the lengths with the sharp edge of a large stone. Somebody had left coal and a few birch logs and I guessed the army or a mountain rescue team with off-road vehicles had recently stayed and billeted the dark rooms. Sure enough, in a cupboard were foil ration-packs and hardtack. I pocketed the biscuits and left the rest. From the burn I filled a large carrier and boiled water for a succession of brews and shared the biscuits, by which time Nick had coaxed the wood-burner to a fine roar. Warmth filled the small room and we slouched back each in a tatty armchair that had once cushioned paying guests at the hunting lodge six miles downriver.

A sluffing sound from above. Snow was sliding from our warmed metal roof and the sliding went on randomly all evening until all was shed. Over lengths of string we draped garments and after two nights in the fridge of the schoolhouse we thawed and clicked our legs straight so that the bare soles of our feet stayed close to the hot metal. Mine had a polished look, Nick's were a little swollen and the sole of one had a kind of ruddy excrescence. Later a dry gale got up and strafed the roof and we could hear waves leap along the shoreline and see the faint gleam of ice slabs heaped up at the outflow like glaziers' refuse. Clive's presence was strong here. I thought about the special allegiance he seemed to have for this hideaway, a man who loved a crowd yet also loved to go alone to the hills. As if to conjure him up we spoke his name and on the back of this came his laugh and easy nature. We matched times with friends and every retelling needed a new canvas and in this lonely place I was reminded acutely of what we'd lost. The sharing of hill days that ran through my adult life, a thread unbroken until now.

'To have that suddenly wrenched from you,' I said, 'is like losing part of your own history. What you lived and relived many times over is now gone, just a collection of private thoughts.'

Nick was quiet. I thought he'd almost relaxed. He opened the stove door and set a piece of old root on the embers and for a moment we listened to it sizzle, then I shared a story about Clive coming here. A decade or so ago, late spring. This time he'd brought along a friend from the city. Their walk-in was marked by a number of dead deer close to the track, not surprising after the winter though each creature's demise appeared to have been very recent. All had been scavenged to some extent. Clive's friend had come to fish and on the first morning he scoured the lochshore for a likely spot while Clive climbed the slope towards Seana Bhraigh. On such a warm day he had no intention of making the summit but on reaching the small and secluded corrie loch he lounged there in the sun, skimming the odd stone, gazing up at the snow-rimmed corrie. After his picnic he began to leisurely retrace his steps, following the burn that fed into the loch as he'd done on his way up. A few gnarled trees still grew on the steep banks, the only trees for miles. By an old sycamore he was stopped in his tracks. He remembered the tree from the morning but now just ahead was something red and raw. Another dead hind, this one freshly slain. Its neck torn and eviscerated. The poor thing had defecated in fright. How had he missed it on the way up? But he hadn't. A thought occurred that his presence might have disturbed the butchery. He looked about warily. An exposed peat bank nearby held no clue. No tracks on the soft surface. Down by the water's edge some ten minutes away his friend was casting, time and again, his right arm lifting and waving and his line quicksilver on the loch. Not once did he look up. It was eerily quiet. Clive returned to the bothy early and in the long twilight they had an idea to lie in wait close to the kill-site to see what might return, but they didn't. They watched from the door of the bothy and saw nothing that broke the stillness, heard nothing save the wind. Clive was not one to exaggerate and as a journalist liked to get his facts straight. Perhaps he had seen the future.

Going outside for a last time I watched the darkness, the corrie and vague outline of encompassing hills, the scene in essentials unchanged from when I'd first set eyes on it, yet I knew that to be an illusion. The watchers had changed, everything had changed.

It might be that being holed-up in a bothy prolonged Nick's preparation, as if the greater space added a layer of complexity. Last night he'd allowed his gear to wander and I was only aware of it by morning when he attempted to restore order. Howls of frustration now as he rifled each pile for a lost knife or pan lid. He was very particular about a small pouch in which he kept things like his penknife, wallet, lighter, spare batteries, a kind of reliquary, and he wouldn't or couldn't progress until each item was safely stowed against its neighbour.

The morning ticked by. I read a good chunk of my book. When I looked outside cloud was down and snow falling from the north and on the water floes of grey ice being blown corrie-wards to bottleneck at the far end. The only way to the sanctuary of Glenbeg was to traverse Seana Bhraigh, all three thousand feet of it. Nick fretted about the ascent. He said it wasn't the day to be climbing hills. He was right, it wasn't, but we had little choice. Glenbeg was but a staging post. We had food buried by Loch Glascarnoch and we needed to reach it within the next two days, three at the most.

In late morning gloom the path skirting the east side of the loch was all but under water and the river at its egress had to be waded. We veered up for a burn that poured nosily from the upper corrie, keeping to ground blown free of snow and passing solitary trees of advanced age, their boughs creaking with each pulse of wind. After a while we angled for the main shoulder, again treading where snow was thinnest, and climbed until reaching the cloudbase. I leaned against the wind and waited. Nick's wraith-like figure was some way behind, moving slowly, and I began to worry at our halting progress. The bothy we'd left just an hour ago looked puny from here, a tiny square half-seen then gone altogether in mist and snow eddying over the dark loch. At the ridge the wind greeted us all the stronger and at a small frozen loch we paused to brandish axes. We carried no crampons. Above us rose the mountain's high defences and I knew the approach to be steep. Protruding rocks enamelled in ice as were our jackets. Nick stamped about with his weapon and frosted face like a worker in a meat-store. Bypassing the cliffs we swung north onto old frozen snow, so hard and wind-shorn we had to swung our axes for footings and so strong the wind we crossed the final slopes stooped and meandering. At the small summit cairn I crouched to fix a bearing. Nick stood at some remove from the cliff face that dropped sheer into the mist, without which we had little sense of our elevation, a wild hill-top in the Highlands a long way from anywhere. For a time we ploughed a slope of faultless white, spindrift hissing past on its southerly tract until the land steepened and lichened rocks again surfaced and below us and west were crags rimming the depths of Cadha Beag, a forgotten and isolated valley of which we steered well clear. By small degrees we saw further ahead, the contours and irregular form of land softened by snow and from this a broader scene emerged. A frozen lochan offered us a waypoint and then the dark twisting line of the burn steered us into the bowl of the valley and we landed by the river flats still some way from the bothy. Snow came from the north in squalls and in those few minutes we saw little save ourselves and walked only to the compass's needle. A familiar gash in the valleyside loomed on our right, dark and jaw-like. When Nick caught me up I pointed it out and said there was not far to go.

Drifting snow had narrowed the river and each mid-channel rock had grown an apron of ice and each had a frozen tail, pendants worn by the bitter waters. Hanging from the undercuts and exposed banks were ice tines, rows of strange piping like something crafted to be tuneful. I stopped to study one but was shoved forward by the wind. The valley broadened and through the fog of drifting snow ahead I began to make out a shape, the old cottage. Again I reassured Nick. A mile, I said, no more. The wind was less and a wan moon appeared suspended overhead to show the way. I counted the years since my last visit, five I thought, four and ten months to be exact, and I remembered who with.

I knew the Mountains Bothies Association no longer maintained the place so wasn't sure what to expect. The door had been left unbolted and was slightly ajar. I pushed and it got caught in a small drift that had built up in the porch. With the latrine spade I scraped away snow and tried to shut the door behind us but it wouldn't sit properly in its frame so I jammed it with a weight. An air of neglect hung about the interior. A table, some chairs, a bucket for cinders, a broken broom. On the mantelpiece two candle-holders cut from beercans lay in a coagulant of wax. Last year's visitors had left a little wood foraged from bog or river. I touched a piece. Pretty dry. With a rusty saw in the storeroom I set about cutting it to lengths that would fit the hearth while Nick made brews and cleared out the fireplace. He set up a small pyramid of kindling and charcoal and within an hour had concocted a fine blaze. We ate dinner steaming in its warmth. Nick cupped his third or fourth brew and sat before the flames like some primate and was generally much cheered. He'd cleaned a couple of old pots and now proceeded to pack them with snow and set his bare feet one in each and winced and breathed noisily through his teeth but said it was worth it for the relief it brought.

It snowed for much of the night and by morning spindrift lay inches deep in the small hallway. The brightness outside was misleading, the land so much whiter. A three-foot drift had risen by the west gable. Looking across to where yesterday the river flowed was now largely a waste of snow, the waters reduced or gone altogether and its banks marked only by the uppermost spikes of rush and these blown flat with each gust.

Nick was up making a brew. There wasn't much to discuss. The promised blizzard had arrived and we weren't going anywhere. Standing about in the cold though was not an option and after breakfast I went to work in the storeroom with the blunt saw and an old pick and chipped away at a tree stump someone had dragged there. I thought if I worked hard I could stay warm, either that or I crawl back into my sleeping pit. I carried the bits to Nick in the main room where he ranked the lumber dry or damp, palming each fragment and studying it like someone at a market stall, then he ran his knife over the chosen piece to produce shavings. Slow and methodical, it reminded me of how he sorted his gear every morning.

Sometime around noon and during a lull in the falling snow we trenched a path upriver to where I knew a series of ditches ran among the peat and poking from their sides the footings of a long dead forest. Snow plumed from the ridge above the bothy and we walked slowly and when reaching the banks tramped along the depressions, kicking at drifts. It seemed a little futile but then Nick called over. He'd found something. With his gloved hands he dug down until a grey and knarly thing emerged, part of root system. It was manacled solidly to the earth and we had to wrench at it, the timber coming apart with a whiff of resin that even in the wind reached us from its peat prison after what might be thousands of years. One piece snapped and threw me in the snow and Nick stood over me laughing. Laden and bent we struggled back and debated whether we had sufficient for the night and a little for the next visitors. After soup and brews and perhaps for want of something to do we braved the outside again, this time walking bowed into a blizzard and were only able to see ahead for brief moments and more than once I thought we should turn back. This time I carried the pickaxe and Nick a crowbar, and so armed we appeared ready to face and do combat with some enemy from the north rather than to collect a little firewood. I worked on a piece too large to lug home, the snow coming in so thick I could hardly see and I swung the pick half blind and sometimes missed. A few yards downwind Nick was clouting with his crowbar. He worked with an intensity I'd rarely seen, levering apart the grain to reveal sinews of deep amber and I couldn't help but feel this action of ours was a kind of butchery, at least of plunder, of what had matured in prior summers, to be carted off and burnt and reduced to ashes.

Light was failing as we crammed into our sacs what we could and turned for our return, the wind and snow hammering at our backs. Nick was shouldering a large wedge of timber like the mandible from a giant insect and he wobbled as he walked and in the maelstrom I could see neither river nor slope and trudging back my one thought was we could easily miss the bothy. On the slope across the river were a group of about a dozen deer standing motionless against the blizzard, as forlorn as wild beasts can appear, each alone from their neighbour and all waiting out the storm and accepting what the night might bring.

The square of the bothy loomed, briefly but enough for me readjust my direction, then a great yowling behind was Nick, stuck fast in a drift. He shouted, saying his feet had gone through to some underlayer of swamp. The more he struggled the greater his entanglement and he roared with frustration. On hands and knees I scooped away snow then great palmfuls of slush but still the bog held him. With great restraint I applied the pick and cleared a space around each boot until inch by inch he lifted one out then the other, each coming with a great plopping sound and he rolled and lay on his back and laughed and shouted with relief. In a few minutes though he'd fallen in again. He'd disappeared behind a small ridge of snow, though not entirely as I could see the crown of his balaclava nodding as he tried to free himself. I offered to carry the great root. No, he wouldn't let me, and anyhow there was just yards to go.

The day was all but gone, it being hardly a day. Inside the old cottage with snow now covering the back windows it was darker still. Nick slumped heavily into the only chair. I sat on the bench and in ten minutes began to shiver. This was no good so I went to work in the storeroom, sawing and splitting, my tools blunt and the wood yielding only to brute strength. The door latch had gone so the door couldn't be closed and everything was covered in a fine snow like talc. Even in the constant frost the room had a faint earthy smell, of damp and rot, a legacy of neglect. I toiled away at our haul and kept the cold at bay and at intervals brought wood to Nick for sorting. With a final load I found him sat with a steaming mug of tea to hand and on his lap a piece of wood over which he passed his knife. So utterly absorbed, I thought. He looked up. 'There's hot water in the pan,' he said.

In both corners were neat piles of wood graded dry to wet and in which order they would be used. The fire was slow. An hour at least before I stopped shivering and felt any warmth but thereafter it radiated a kind of magic and transformed the shabby interior. Our last candle guttering and the bothy and its spare furnishings now lit solely by what flared in the hearth. Surfaces took on a brassy light, soft shadows played on the ceiling and wainscot. Nick quiet, bent firewards, chin resting in his hands. Sizzle and pop of old resin. The heat from suns that reigned above Gleann Beag thousands of years ago. When I spoke I said I thought those deer wouldn't last the night, at any rate there would be casualties and it was a cruel irony that they would die among the roots of an old forest. Trees that might have once offered sanctuary. Nick said he reckoned the deer survive most winters and that there's always plenty come spring.

'Only the ones that can get shelter,' I said, 'but it's all open out there. Nowhere the wind can't reach.'

'It's even coming in under the door,' Nick said, looking behind him, 'and bringing the snow with it. Anyhow, I thought the owner of this estate is a confirmed protector of nature?'

'So he claims. I've read he's overseen the planting of thousands of native trees in a bid to recreate the old woods, which is all great, though tree-planting fever has yet to reach the really remote places. Here for instance. This glen is as moribund as ever.'

'Didn't he want to fence his land and bring back wolves and bears?'

'Yes, he did, maybe still does. Freedom to Roam legislation put a stop to that one. He might have saved himself a few quid had he bothered to read the Statute Book. This land is for everyone, not just millionaires and their pet projects, however worthy.'

Nick stooped to blow at the fire, not that he needed to.

'I thought his argument for bringing back wolves was to restore the natural balance,' Nick said. 'A closely monitored wolfpack to cull the deer and allow native woodland to regenerate. Wolves are apex predators. Their presence benefits the entire ecosystem. They put it back in sync. It's only recently we've realised the value of such predators in the regulatory role and how they maintain bio-diversity. There are many examples. Restoring the balance is not about fulfilling some romantic vision of the Highlands that might have existed in the past but is crucial for long term sustainability. It's that important. The Highlands will overall remain denuded but repairing one small corner is better than nothing. Surely?'

'All true, but you forget he also wanted to create a kind of safari park with guides, 4x4 vehicles, paying guests.'

I studied the heap of wet wood and leaned across it and picked out a piece, round like a pipe and black with earth. I placed one end onto the blaze and give it a quick shunt. Orange flames and a flurry of sparks as it settled. Nick was staring intently at the fire. I said that bringing wolves back as some sort of business venture even in part reflects an attitude that has brought us to the brink of environmental ruin. It's one of arrogance and maybe took shape when we started farming, in particular when we started farming livestock. I said up to that point we'd had a hand in altering our environment and it's true we caused extinctions but now it's all about management. The control of living matter. It's costing us the earth, I said. Scientists are calling it the Anthropocene. The Sixth Great Extinction. Not a prediction but a reality. It's happening this minute.

With his eyes still firmly on the blaze Nick said the guy who owns this plot is probably just trying to do the right thing.

'As he sees it?'

'Of course "as he sees it". How else?'

'So we're happy to bring these creatures back but we want everything on our terms. We'll corral them into enclosures and if they put a paw outside we'll shoot them. Plenty in the hunting crowd would pay for that pleasure. In Norway recently the government declared the few dozen wolves still left in the wild were too many and plans a cull. Gun-owners were invited to apply for a special wolf-culling license. Thousands did so.'

'Yeah. I read that and it surprised me. But it shows the ignorance of tradition.'

'A park is one step from a zoo,' I said. 'If we can only save a wild animal by cooping it up or making it perform or by freezing its embryos in some laboratory then let's not bother. Zoos are run by folk who believe sincerely in their worth, but who wants to see a wild creature in a cage or paraded before a crowd? I can't see how that helps their plight, in fact it engenders an attitude that the earth's creatures somehow exist solely for us. We have to think differently.'

'It would be cruel to the wolf to bring it back before we are ready. There have to be impact studies, public and stakeholder consultations, a political will. And top of the list, an area large and remote enough for them to thrive. The lynx will probably need to come first. It's not the answer but might be a stepping-stone for the wolf.'

I looked at my peat-grimed hands in the firelight, turning them, and wondered if I'd ever get them clean again.

'That all sounds calm and reasonable but you've kind of made my point,' I said.

Nick shrugged and didn't respond. The fire made a low blowing sound.

'I believe they will come back,' I said. 'And probably sooner than you think. But let them come with no fanfare. Just set aside plenty of room for them to wander. Far from them being a menace to farmers, they might actually be our saviour.'

With its deepset windows and persistent gloom and fireplace still with a soot-caulked chain hanging from the darkness the cottage recalled an atmosphere of an earlier time. Under the table was a hotchpotch of blackened and dented pots and kettles, most gone to rust, and in the other room stashes of nails, screws, metal sheeting, the paraphernalia of patch and repair carted in over the hill when this remote building was routinely maintained. I couldn't say how much longer the bothy would provide shelter, the only such for miles, the old place now subject to a slow and ceaseless attrition, fingers of unseen rot in the panelling fed by constant damp, windward walls loosened and invaded in this corridor of gales and inclemency. Whatever we build, time will undo. That evening by the fire we were a witness to it. Water in slow drips, snow under a door that wouldn't close and on another day I guess pooling rain here would drown a sleeping mouse. No one comes now to fix and fortify, not even a local with a liking for wild places. There are no locals, this spot so remote any patch-up would take a weekend at least.

In time a ruin is all that will stand, a crumbling memorial for the hundreds who have stayed ever since its restoration half a century ago. Maybe its final years will be the best. Half-haunted in its twilight, the door gone and windows out and falling timbers making each stay perilous, huddled in the keep of the last room, the furnishings and panels long since stripped, smashed, burnt, the guts of the bothy disappearing in an act of self-consumption. One winter and seen by deer a mile away a rising pall of slate-dust as the last section of roof caves in. The final abandonment, the place forsaken even by its ghosts.

Folk passing still pause and some will bed down by the lichened walls on that strip of jade enriched by generations, they knowing something of its history or just curious. Among the rubble now grow heather and ferns and a young rowan flown from the ravine and happy in its niche of leaching lime. With the passing into history of Glenbeg shieling fewer will find their way to this trackless valley leading only to a wild high country and to nowhere.

The west gable honed the wind and we listened to it rising and sat and talked and watched the fire die for a long time, glowing coals gridlined, limbs awry. I saw in its heart other fires and remembered how a fire provided not only warmth but a key to the unlocking of memories, faces bright like clowns and creased with laughter and one among them bespectacled and expressing some inner ease and laughing loudest, recounting the good from the day, an aura unconsciously free of self so that even the strangers by the fire could drop their guard and remember. I always thought he made the old tales better, funnier. He spun them out like snares of silk. He could see what few saw, that most human ventures were in fact comedies, and true to his calling he reported them as such.

Six

I slept in the far room and if any warmth had reached it from the fire then by morning it had gone. Frost on the ceiling, the air dense with cold. The one small window had grown strange ferns and when I loosened my drawcord to listen I heard just the sieving wind. I thought the cold in general was a good sign. I reached for my socks, wet, half-frozen. In my clothes bag was a dry pair but I was saving them. For what? With my boots on I clumped to the door and scraped away the snow that had come in underneath during the night and walked out into a bright clean world. Sunshine roamed the valley in great searchlights and when I looked up I squinted and felt its vague warmth. The snowy land seemed much altered. Some aspects and ridge crests had been combed clear while all burn lines seemed choked and a cornice on the ravine above the bothy wore a trailing cloak. The drift by the storeroom now chest high and the rough exterior masonry grouted with blown snow.

Nick had largely packed the night before and only a little of the morning had gone when we ploughed the valley drifts and angled for the watershed to the west. I broke trail and broke through a surface rippled into tiny ridges and over this an almost constant transfer of spindrift. The climb was steep. Our home of two nights became lost in the dead ground but our visual orbit grew. The valley that had walled us in now extended east for ten miles, a great carved trench narrowing at each spur and holding a ribbon of water that curled many times until lost in the pinewoods of Alladale. We walked west and after another rise Cona Mheall broke the alpine sky like the roof of a great ice tepee. There was joy where the night winds had driven the snow thinly and we could move with ease, our steps supported, or the wind had packed the surface so hard it was like sand released by an ebb tide and we crossed in quickstep, jauntily. Hard wet acres in summer now refigured into a frozen highway and our transit in the second hour was such that Nick begun to sing. It couldn't last. The snow removed from the high country had to be somewhere. I felt the breeze on my back and watched a column of snow eddy and tear off downhill and vanish.

Keeping above the watershed we edged the frozen hollow of Loch Prille and here the weather closed in again. At the headwall of the loch's outflow and where a waterfall spouted from a great drift we became engulfed in blowing snow. The land fell away in outcrops and we picked our way down blindly and at times I could barely see Nick who was just yards away.

At the base of the headwall and reaching the first of three lochs, Loch na Stil, the wind had largely died. I took out the map to thumb the promised miles. Our food lay buried close to Loch Glascarnoch, some four miles by our route and now with little by way of descent. But much of the snow that had fallen over the previous days now so clogged this south-trending valley I thought we would struggle to cover the miles before dark. Nick insisted on breaking trail and led off, feet splayed and his route guesswork about the boulderfields and his heavier frame sinking sometimes two feet or more. After a few minutes he stopped and turned and said he preferred if I followed behind at some remove. He couldn't say why, only that he felt somehow pressured. I said I didn't think I was so close and offered to take over trailbreaking duties. Give me until the end of the loch, he said. He stood up and set off with new resolve.

The mile-long Loch Coire Lair filled the valley entirely and the toil on its west bank became our slowest yet, all the land now under a thick blanket. The snow hid unfrozen ground and sometimes we went through to the marshland beneath. Watching our tedious approach was a small group of deer and at some point they began moving upslope, all save for one whose leg was broken, for the creature put no weight on it and stepped slowly and with great effort. The cripple paused and looked over at us and then after its companions, now a quarter mile away. None were waiting.

The loch was part frozen, the wind having shifted the ice from its northern arm and shoved it like a plough to the egress where grey shelvings overlapped. Nick drove on through drifts. I thought his effort remarkable given his slowness coming off Seana Bhraigh two days before. He wasn't quick but he didn't stop and at this rate I thought we might even make our camp before nightfall.

But if anything the snow grew deeper as we worked down-valley, the land hardly falling now. Our workload mounted and Nick allowed me to take the reins. A conveyor-belt of showers funnelled in from the north. During one we hunkered in the lee of a great rock and I ate my remaining tin of fish and Nick the last of his dried fruit. The high ground of the Fannichs began to show ahead, but day was fading and we could see the silent drift of car-lights on the Ullapool road, their engine sound taken by the wind.

Darkness caught us still more than a mile from our cache site and in the gloom the snow took on an ashen and unreckonable texture, the snares it concealed greater than we'd yet encountered, provoking caution and many a detour and I believe our final line to a small wood was double the distance marked yet was the only way. We scouted amongst the pines for a half-adequate space for the tents, the ground under the snow everywhere greatly waterlogged. Nick elected for a raised but uneven spot in the wood's centre. I pitched on the periphery. I shook snow from branches above my site to prevent it coming down during the night. After fixing the shelters we went for the grub. A trail of hooves to follow on the far side of the trees. These led to an area of flattened snow and dung and a musty odour where deer had gathered in the blizzard. Further on I trained my torch on a pair of eyes close to the ground. They were watching us. As we neared they hardly moved until only yards away we saw a deer hind collapsed in the snow, alone and frightened, its little head raised up and twitching, as if throwing off flies. It didn't make the slightest attempt to stand and probably couldn't.

The cache was under a foot of snow, under some rocks, all intact. At Nick's pitch site while tea was brewing I doled out provisions equal by weight and something easy for tonight, tinned chilli con carne with rice, tinned fruit, tinned cream, and with my share I retired to my tent.

I thought after such a day I could sleep through anything, but the thrash of wind in the trees woke me and I sat up to shake the tent of snow. Pitched on the southern ground of the wood I'd felt confident of some protection yet the wind pummelled my small home and snow periodically fell from the limbs in soft thuds. I wondered how Nick was faring. I woke fully, later than usual and to a great hunger, so made double my usual helping of porridge. I thawed my boots over the stove and went over to check on Nick. His tent so paltry, the guys loose and fly sagging under the weight of snow. Despite that, his site in the heart of the wood was well chosen. He must have heard me for as I approached there was the sound of a zip and clank of cookware. His flysheet trembled and Nick's head emerged. He said he'd slept without a single interruption. Dreamless too. What about all that wind and snow? What about it, he said, though my tent does seem smaller. He punched the insides. Snow luffed from the folds to the ground and the tent sprang more into its old shape.

'How are your feet?'

'No better after yesterday's effort.'

'You mean walking for ten hours in the snow didn't improve them?'

'Are you joking?'

'Which one is worse?'

Nick looked back inside his vestibule and thought for a moment.

'Don't know,' he said, 'I'll give them a wiggle. I'm sure they'll tell me.' He made to concentrate for a few seconds. Then seemed baffled. 'Right now I can't honestly say, though I guess it's whatever foot I'm using.'

He poured water into a pan and lit his stove.

'So what d'you reckon?' he said.

'I reckon with all this extra snow overnight we should lay up for a day. Give it a chance to settle. Whatever we do we're looking at an almighty effort to reach the head of Loch Fannich, and then Achnasheen. That's two good days, though more likely three. At least we've plenty of grub.'

Nick rolled back his head to look at the sky. Clouds swift beyond the canopy of spruce and beyond that a blue vault. The sun already eclipsing hills east of the loch and its brightness reaching us through a fretwork of branches.

'Yeah, it's probably a bit late to be heading off,' he said. 'You know, by the time I get my things ready.'

'I'm saying nothing.'

I took his empty canister and trudged off to collect water. The river was a feeder burn and half frozen, grey ice spreading from midstream rocks like freshwater medusas and the waters carrying small floes in a slow drift on the low ground before Glascarnoch reservoir, itself now stilled with ice. I walked to the north side of the wood and marvelled at the prospect. Beinn Dearg, Cona Mheall, Am Faochagach, the great snowfields and scoured ridgelines betraying the winds of the last days.

The frost never lifted. All day snow plumed and found its way into our small wood and covered everything in a fine powder. The air felt bitter and I kept my walks short. In raw afternoon light I studied the Fannichs and eyed a line into one of its corries and thence to the ridge. In outline the folds presented a kind of human form, their faces veined in blue and trailing snow in great grey locks. The wind rose in a flurry of spindrift and I stepped back into the wood for shelter. This planted wood the only mature green in the visible landscape.

Once the Glascarnoch river, tumultuous or idle, ran the empty miles of the strath, cattle-grazing country mostly, the marsh fringes good only for an array of resident birds and in all those miles just a croft or two broke the green and brown weft of moor. A land long ransacked of trees though still lovely for all that, until the engineers and hired muscle came and built the dam at Aultguish and made a shallow loch of the valley, so shallow the acres of mud at its head can now appear like a drained estuary. A sterile one. There is another dam at Strath Vaich and another at Fannich. In high plots south and east of the dam the engineers have now added giant rotating blades to capture the wind. So many turbines have sprung up around Ben Wyvis this lovely brooding hill now seems enclosed by them, an industrial greeting to motorists heading north.

I know someone who laboured on the Fannich Dam, himself a climber and skier among the gangs of navvies and engineers and someone who knew the hills beyond the poured concrete. A proud man and proud of his work, yet his views have softened and he says that at the time he'd not reckoned on the sterility of loch margins. In hindsight he believes too many dams were raised and the present mania for wind-farms in such places is a desecration. But he doubts if they will always be here. In our lifespan yes, but the generations to come will have the stolen views back and hills as they were and that is a good thing.

The heavy snow forced a rethink on the Fannichs. The difficulty was not so much in climbing high, more the lochshores and valleys where the snow had gathered. To reach the far end of Loch

Fannich was no easy matter. The central Fannich ridge rose three thousand feet and the ways over it were few. An obstacle to the westbound traveller. Due south over the low pass to the dam at the mouth of the loch would still leave some eight miles of lochside drifts to plough through. With the map open I talked it through with Nick. He said he wanted to climb high and cross the ridge, the col just north of An Coileachean. We could do that for sure, I said, and from there angle down and cut the lochside march by more than half. Nick nodded, supping his tea and studying the map. He said he couldn't be sure if his battered soles would be a match for the next stage but he was committed to the idea of moving on, even though he'd not always expressed this, at least not verbally. He said the walk had forced upon him a way of living that was beneficial. I said I believed it was the sheer work-rate, the pared down diet, the hard miles and rest. He agreed but added the journeying took him to a place different to where he usually resided. In his head, that is. The winter mountains were uplifting in ways he'd almost forgotten, this being his first big walk for years. This time he would remember and such memories were better than any medicine. I can't be sure about the long-term, he said, but I feel better right now. He spoke this sitting cross-legged in the shelter of his vestibule, hatted and gloved and wearing many layers.

'Living can be a daily struggle,' he said. 'While it might be true that some of my burdens are imagined they are real enough for me and they disrupt what most take for granted. Like the way I pack. For you it's routine that becomes easier the more you do it, a case of fine tuning. I watch you. You hardly have to think and I bet you don't care where stuff goes as long as it fits, as long as you can do it quickly. You might adjust a strap or move something that's poking your back but that's all. It takes you minutes. I envy that. For me every morning I have to deal with random objects that shout chaos. It's not that I've forgotten how to pack or how I did it before, it's just I have a whole load of choices to make over again, even the same choices.'

'Well, in that department I reckon you're speeding up. We were away from the bothy early, remember.'

'That was because I'd sorted my stuff the night before.'

'Yeah, remember those mornings in the north? My hair went grey just waiting. But you're into a routine now, though I'll be honest, you're not exactly fast.'

'I think I'm getting there. I hate to waste time, especially when there are hills to walk. We need to get to Knoydart.'

I heard sometime during the night the slack drip of water. By dawn the ice on my fly had melted and around my tent the snow was wet and heavy. Yesterday's brightness replaced by low cloud which curtained the hills around. No wind to speak of. We crossed the road with snow piled up on both sides and struck up the left side of the burn that drained the West Fannichs, its stranglehold of ice being loosened.

For a time the land barely rose and the going was heavy. We ploughed a narrow corridor between the burn and the bound-ary fence of a young mixed wood of native trees. Being greatly overgrazed this region is barren of trees, so the dwarf groves here are a delight, but as usual the demarcation between land grazed and that protected was striking. Thawing snow made for slow going and it was a while before we left the last corner of wood and ascended southwest, the burn never more than trickling and much of it completely buried. The heavy cloud presence dissipated and slowly the scale of the high Fannichs began to manifest, the spillways on the crags frozen and on one a cascade of ice like the feathered wings of a great bird. A wreath of cloud made the cliffs seem very high and distant.

Away from the burn the snow grew thinner, a place of wind-scour during the blizzard, clipped heather showing on some aspects and the frozen ground below had no give. Oddly we saw two small cairns and thought a path led into the corrie but in a few yards it was hidden by drifts.

The amelioration brought by the warmer air was worrying and it was hard to know to what height the thaw extended. Strong winds over the last days had banked the snow up on certain aspects. A new and uncertain weight on the land and I thought it wouldn't take much to trigger a slide. If we had to climb to the summits and avoid the corries altogether then we would.

The mist lifted enough for us to eye cliffs and a headwall and for a time we saw Bealach Ban and our entryway to the west, a bulge of snow right at its lip. We paused to study it and reckoned on the best line to avoid such a risky build-up. We'd yet to hear the boom of an avalanche but now as we looked into the corrie of Loch Gorm I pointed at a runout of snow blocks like a coastal defence. It had come down from high up on the east of the corrie, perhaps sometime yesterday.

The cliffs across from the loch were divided by great scissoring gullies loaded with blown snow, the loch itself swept clean and the ice on it growing in concentric bands from the shore. We circled above the loch and climbed steeply, pawing for handholds, keeping to exposed rock and heading south as if we were climbing An Coileachan. When more or less in line with the pass and keeping a good distance apart we traversed and trod gingerly, our boots sinking, the snow creaking. I watched the slope below but it seemed solid. The mist wound around us again and almost nothing of a breeze and so quiet we heard the faint clatter of a train, the noise reaching us from over seven miles of hill. Growing then fading like someone beating out a message in morse. If it was the eastbound train then I knew it would soon be dark.

Although cushioning our downward strides we couldn't fathom the depth of fresh snow and proceeded with great slowness, especially Nick who now lagged so behind I could barely see him for the mist, just a vague shape.

The ground grew suddenly steep and I feared for its stability. I thought we may have strayed too far into Coire Riabhach so veered more to the left and more to the fall-line. I went ahead and lost Nick entirely and waited on easier ground at a great perched boulder. He would have no trouble following my prints. As I waited I speculated where such a thing had come from and what had conveyed it, maybe trundled down from the heights or left by a retreating glacier whose antecedents themselves had gouged the trench now filled by Loch Fannich. As light faded the mist lifted somewhat and we could approach slowly the dark loch and a regular group of conifers by the lodge. No lights. The ground levelling now, the snow deeper and baseless and much drifted and sometimes I crashed through to some hollow and twice I fell headlong.

Evenings had lengthened a little since the passing of January but with a heavy cloud presence it was hardly noticed. The light was gone and wouldn't come again for another sixteen hours.

I'd hoped to make the old refuge of the Nest but now didn't think it likely. The weariness of a day in the snow. There was a track by the lodge but I knew our reaching it wouldn't make much difference. The going could hardly have been slower. In the middle distance on a ridge a line of deer in silhouette, dark shapes on a grey land and all their heads raised and so still they might have been fashioned from bronze. When Nick stood beside me there was barely any light and when he asked I had to admit there were four or so miles still to cover.

I was familiar with the track but it was buried and its line unclear. Two or three times we blundered onto the moor. It was hardly better with our torches and outwith our beams it was darker still. The track stole landwards and climbed and this section so heavily drifted I had to lean into the snow and pummel it with my knees like a strange penance. Then I thought I could smell smoke. A woodfire at the Nest? But the Nest was gone and at any rate there was no breeze. My memory playing tricks.

The plantation was just ahead and I knew the drifts there would be even worse. My beam caught the rough surface of a boulder. I waited. Nick's wavering light wasn't far in arrears.

'Let's camp,' I said when he caught up.

'What, here?'

'Yes, why not?'

'Thought you were keen to reach the Nest?'

'I am, but it'll still be there tomorrow. What's left of it.'

'What is left of it?'

'Well, there's no roof.'

'Small detail that. Not really a house then, is it?'

'I never said it was.'

'You didn't say it was a ruin either.'

'I slept in the pony shed on my last visit.'

'Either way not much of a lure. What about our schedule? Thought you said two days to Achnasheen?'

'Still possible, though we'll need a frost.'

'I don't see any stars.'

'I know. Could it be any darker? So, are we going to clear this ground for our tents?'

'Okay.'

The air was so still that each word we spoke came back in a soft echo and Nick called our camp Echo Rock. Using my plate as a kind of shovel I proceeded to clear away snow and it took some time. The soft turf beneath made for sound peg placements. I cooked a meal for myself and wrote no more than a few words and said little across the divide to Nick, just asking whether he'd given his feet ice baths and what he was planning to cook, for I'd not heard the odd tantrum that could accompany the operation.

There was no frost and the slow thaw continued and in the first grey light I saw dark streaks on some of the hill-flanks. The high ground of the Fannichs again was entirely lost in mist. Nick was most of the morning packing his sac, then not an hour into our walk and having entered the wood of pine and spruce he called a halt. He sat down and removed his boots and socks and packed snow around his bare feet. All this he did with barely any expression. I asked how it felt. Great, he said.

I didn't think we'd get far. As expected the forest trail was deeply snowed and when we emerged into the open again the loch had narrowed and I knew the Nest would soon be in view. In wistful mood I led, for I'd not approached the Nest this way for many years.

Long dark miles through a December evening and leaning hard into a west wind and it was about here, I remembered, that we'd begun to smell woodsmoke, just snatches at first then stronger, as if a great fire was abroad, the air thick with it. I recall the two of us waiting outside the house, unsure. Smoke belching from the east chimney and leached from the open door like some fumarole. I pushed at the door and another to the hallway and yet another to a room with voices. Inside a group sat on boxes and a crude bench huddled by the hearth and in the smoky dimness they seemed a gathering of conspirators. One of their number with his back to us had both arms around the end of a great trunk he was feeding into the blaze. When he turned to speak I could make out only the twin discs of his spectacles. Like copper coins hanging there in the dark. Then I saw his teeth.

All this and other details I recalled for Nick as the track turned and dropped and here the snow had been swept clear and at last we could stretch and walk with a little ease. The Nest became visible on the near skyline, forlorn, a ruin this last quarter century. A willow still clung to the ground in front and some pines occupied a knoll behind, planted a long time ago to soften the corrie winds. I knew the Nest in its last years when two of its rooms were always locked. I always visited in winter. The best base from which to explore the high crests and corries of the Fannichs.

I stood in the snow and on the threshold of what used to be the porch and realised I'd been here more during its dereliction than when it functioned as a bothy. I was here a month or so after the burning and twenty-five years later there is still charred wood and signs of scorch. Still a tangle of rusting iron. The bedstead, I thought. The empty doorway leading to a roofless space, the rooms and floors gone, no upstairs and all open to the sky. I was surprised the walls still retained their full height though maybe not for long. Mortar was loose to touch and came away easily and in crevices coarse grass and moss had colonised. Time and the reckoning of gravity are no match for such neglect. On the grass-grown floor were sheets of corrugated iron and part of the firegrate. Clay shards from the chimney pot. I looked through the gaps where the windows had been. A snowy landscape, the great flanks of hills to the north cold and bleak, the narrow palette of a winter's day.

I think I'd first gone to the hills out of some compulsion. The seed of it being family camping trips and journeys in a small sailing craft, guided by parents who in their quiet way exampled an appetite for adventure, something beyond our local common and a large park with gates and curfew. The engineered urban space I'd grown up in was an ill fit. You walk corridors made by others and you walk through dog-waste and chimney-smoke and the smell of exhausts and metallic taste of dust, the breeze from the pissed-in alleys like a foul breath and all through the starless dark a growl of trucks and trains and garish lights of jumbos passing in their flight-lanes, fixed and encumbered. Not like birds. Maybe I saw too much its dark side but looking back I thought it wasn't just that. Emerging from the sheer plod of school onto society's conveyor and into a straitjacket of work and expectation, replacing one set of rules for another, I was caught somehow between loathing and desire, the small-minded snob-beries of suburbia and the bright uplands, imagined and real.

Standing by the walls I remembered again that first trip with Dave Hughes, our first Hogmanay in the hills. A group of climbers and walkers from Fort William around the fire and tales from the world's wilder corners, travel and adventures in the Great Ranges. They spoke of austral winters and sleeping under foreign constellations and sang and drank and one of their number was poorly and had come in by vehicle and hardly stirred from his bed, a young man, a fine climber of rock and ice they said. I read in a magazine he died soon after. The obituarist wrote that the day he died was one of torrential rain and the rain was tears for this man.

Daylight hours were spent climbing to the Fannich ridge and tracing its crest and outriders. On the third day we'd been on the horseshoe of Sgurr Breac and A'Chailleach and were chased

Camp on the north coast at the beginning of our walk, Tongue Bay in the distance.

Descending Ben Hutig.

Approaching Ben Hee from the east.

Crossing the Allt na Claise Moire.

At the head of Loch a' Ghriama and a distant Loch Shin.

Afternoon shadows on the climb to the hills of the Cassley Basin.

A perishing morning in the Assynt Basin.

The ruin of Tubeg, by Loch Assynt and Quinag.

Leaving Suilven and heading south-east.

Loch Gorm and Creag Dubh a' Gorm Locha in the Fannichs.

Sunrise on Sgurr a'Bhealaich Dheirg. A view from Camban bothy.

Waterfall in Coire Chorsalain.

Looking down Loch Hourn to Ladhar Bheinn and Barrisdale Bay.

A last descent east along Loch Hourn to our final camp.

Ladhar Beinn from the north shore of Loch Hourn.

Clive on the summit of Beinn a' Chreachain, April 2012.

home by a blizzard. It snowed that night and was still snowing by morning, though lightly. A cue for the Fort William crowd to pack and leave. A vehicle for the lying man came while it could. We stayed on. It snowed the next night and through the next day, a blizzard coming from the east and obliterating the loch. Though happy in our incarceration we'd run out of food and with the storm finally passed we were on the track an entire day, flogging through drifts to reach the railway. We sat in the carriage and reeked of woodsmoke, and returned the following year.

I heard again their talk, their singing, scrape of boots on wooden floors. The only shelter here now was the pony shed, no door but still with a roof. When I looked in a dead hind lay on the cobbled floor. A bullet hole in its midriff. A message from the estate perhaps. Maybe from a culture as well. That the stranger is unwelcome, and that there is no obligation for the paper owners of this vast estate to provide even a crude shelter for wayfarers, and why encourage visitors other than those who pay to be here, hunters with rifle and rod?

I took my stove out and boiled water for soup and gave a cup to Nick who was sitting on a rock with his headphones. He took the cup and nodded. I thought of how back then I loved the empty wildness of the Fannichs, a visceral love and antidote to much in my life at the time. I was largely innocent of the ecological and human story that had created this emptiness though such facts anyhow would have withered in the great vistas and joy of wild living. The land spoke to me on a profound level. But even in those early ignorant days I had a sense something wasn't right, an impression of life here being limited, the land I so loved beset by paucity and sickness. I saw few birds and no native trees, a place moribund and the ground species in a narrow spectrum, a pattern largely repeated across the Highlands. A veneer of wildness only. In my years of coming here the estate owners had chipped away even at this, mainly in the bulldozing of a road on the far side of the loch and the muddy scars of all-terrain vehicles. I wondered what they were trying to achieve. Or why rich men buy such lands in the first place. There was no vision here and not much clue.

With the snow unmarked by anything other than deer and small creatures of the moor I doubted if anyone had been here for at least a week. A remote place at the best of times, cornered on three sides by hills. The good path climbs north and bisects the main Fannich watershed and after many rough miles reaches the Dundonell road. We followed the path albeit briefly, the way buried by drifts, and we left it at the first burn and ploughed the flat lands at the head of the loch, the water level at its winter highmark. Picking our way with great care amongst ditches and collapsing snowbridges and wading easily the Abhnain Nid which drains the high hook of hills and which I feared had risen overnight but hadn't. We rounded the head of the loch and paused at a boulder about the size of a van that wore a coronet of heather and we looked back over the grey loch, the ruined house only a few hundred yards away. I said to Nick that during that blizzard all those years ago this stone went unseen for hours and its appearance or not was a kind of herald. The morning after the storm it stood in angled sunshine like a block of white marble.

A little further on we found a newly made track, wide enough for a small-wheeled vehicle, and as we stole west I began to notice fresh treadmarks. The tyres had bitten deep and there were gouts of muddied slush where they had struggled for purchase. Not a mile up the valley we met the vehicle on its return and from a distance it looked like a fairground dodgem, a plaything for adults. Two men in their later years dressed in fatigues and in the back a red deer hind slumped and bloody. The man behind the wheel hailed us and was immediately friendly and admitted to being surprised to see anyone out in such conditions. Worst snows in five years, he said and the poor beasts of the hills were suffering greatly. He'd been the stalker on the estate for many decades and there was barely a yard of it he didn't know. Yes, he remembers the Nest as a standing house like yesterday. He related something of its history. We listened politely and without prompting he spoke of its demise by fire on account of a careless visitor and how it couldn't be saved. He said the estate owners decided the insurance money would not be used to restore the building but on constructing a narrow track along the south side of the loch, money wisely spent in his opinion. I said it was a shame there was no longer any shelter for walkers in such wild country. He seemed bemused at this. Did folk not carry tents, he said. You two look like you know what you're about. The other man stayed silent. A pleasant encounter and we were cheered by it. Their motor noise faded and we continued and I remembered something I'd not asked the stalker. Probably because I'd seen no profit in it. He was the stalker, not the owner, and his opinion only that. Some years ago I was part of a group who were looking to establish a bothy in memory of a friend killed while serving in the RAF during the Kosovan conflict of the late nineties. They had considerable funds, a ready band of volunteers and the blessing of all. Their early enquires identified a number of ruins, one of which was the Nest of Fannich. They were refused permission. Nick listened to the tale.

'You offered to rebuild it, pay for it, the lot?' he said.

'Yes, we had everything ready, funds, promised air support from the RAF and plenty of willing helpers. We just needed a green light.'

'Why did they refuse? I would think a building here would benefit the estate, you know, shelter for their employees, a place to hunker down. Even just to communicate information for walkers and climbers on stalking times and access. There's a lot of confusion out there about access during the hunting season.'

'All true. It was an opportunity lost.'

Nick stopped to tug at a loose chest-strap.

'Maybe they were worried a bothy would attract more folk to a remote corner,' he said.

'How is that a bad thing?'

'It's not, but it might be for them.'

'How so?'

'Disturbance of deer, I guess. This is a traditional estate with paying guests.'

'That's an outdated attitude. Look at the scale of this place. Such a vast area and managed solely for its hunting potential. You could reimagine it as a haven for wildlife and people alike. Just think of that, a beacon of restoration that went some way to redress the great harm we've done the earth. There'd be more people here as well. But if the laws don't change the owner will be able to pass it on to his or her children or sell it to the highest bidder.'

'You're dreaming again.'

'Yes, I am.'

After maybe a couple of miles of hard going we began eying the river for a place to ford. Down at the head of the loch it was impassable but here it was narrower. Ice congealing the peaty water to an ochreous tinge and its depth impossible to judge. I stepped in wearing my old pair of socks. The ice squeaked and collapsed and I stood in two foot of freezing water. I turned and swore at Nick. To make progress I had to lift each foot from the river and bring down my heel hard on the ice and by the end both feet were sore and blue with cold. With his plastic crocs Nick waded through the now floating slabs.

'Thanks,' he said.

'Don't thank me. There's a bigger river to cross tomorrow and you'll be going first.'

'You just have to ask,' Nick said, rubbing his feet.

With less than an hour before dark we came to a disused sheep fank, its old dyking ridged in grass and ling and patterned in lichen, the colours of an underwater reef, a late vibrancy in the grey afternoon. I leaned against a wall waiting. Nick come slowly around a terrace and when I suggested we stop for the night he looked at the dykework and said he couldn't think of a good reason to push on. And these walls have stood for a long time. We dug down more than a foot and cleared tent-shaped spaces and

sunk our pegs easily, the points of each biting into the river gravels that floored the old enclosure. A naturally dry site well known
by the first shepherds though now a remote spot and seldom seen.

Our neighbouring hill of Meallan Chuaich rose almost
unblemished, white fading to inky blue as a slow darkness fell
and later I was a witness to constellations that burned among the
stretched clouds in their transit about the polestar. I remade the
nap of my head-cushion and lay with my head to the west and
studied the map by torchlight and wondered at the absence of
placenames, why the map's architects had failed to name the pass
to the west nor the one to the north, here just a web of burns and
looping contours. Perhaps the names were local only and now
lost. I knew the pass to the north and remembered a summer
when I'd camped there with a friend. We'd reached the pass late
and very tired and decided to put up our tents. In his haste my
friend fixed his flysheet inside out and none of his guys could
be fastened. I said I didn't think it would be a problem. Fine
weather had accompanied our walk and the prior night was still
and swept with stars. We retired to our separate nylon chambers.
I was woken in the dark by someone or something violently
shaking the tent. It was only the vanguard. A dry gale bore down
from the north and our pass took the brunt and amongst its
booming my friend's voice, an octave higher, imploring I do
something about the certain collapse of his tent. I yelled back
that he hold his main supporting pole. For the remainder of the
night if need be. From then on I slept but fitfully, aware of wind
and a nearby voice rising in strange unison with each passing
gust, a commentary on the dark and a curse on me.

Seven

My vestibule at first light framed a valley free of mist, the clouds squatting in the gap between the eastern hills rose-tinted, but I never saw the sun. Overcast again as we climbed due south to a small watershed on the shoulder of Beinn nan Ramh. There was no frost in the snow and we couldn't hurry. Gaining a high point we crested and the far west came in view, a huge arc of quartz and sandstone scenery, Slioch emerging through mist and Beinn Eighe draped like a great white tent and Beinn Tarsuinn and Coire Mhic Fearchair brooding as truncate cones of extinct volcanoes. A corridor of wild mountains that stretched from Garve on the slopes of Ben Wyvis to the west coast some two dozen miles away. The snow-cover presented it entirely unblemished and though a false picture, here I thought was something imagined for the future.

A long descent on the south flank by a burn cascading with melt, the snow here softer yet and choking every lateral gully and we crossed each with great care, hearing in some deep gurgling. Even from a mile away the river in Strath Chrombuill looked swollen, a bright ribbon of energy down there in the valley. We reached it at a point of great turmoil, floodwaters rubbing against its banks, dropping over shelves and coursing among rocks. Just downstream were no rocks but there it was wide and fast and with every passing minute rising that bit higher. How deep it was in the middle I could not tell.

Nick looked over the torrent. 'What are our options?'

'We could track the bank up to the watershed.'

'How far?'

'Miles.'

'And in this snow. What about the other way?'

'Miles again. And it would only get us to Kinlochewe, assuming all the sidestreams were fordable.'

'And if not?'

'Then we won't be eating tonight.'

Nick again ran his eyes across the river.

'So what do you think?' he said.

'You know what I think.'

'Here?'

'Yes.'

If Nick vacillated of a morning over what item belonged in what pocket of his rucksack, I watched him now sit and begin to remove his boots and socks and all his lower garments. Let's do it, he said, we haven't got long. But you go first. I didn't argue. I tied my boots together, slung them over one shoulder. I unbelted my rucksack and stepped into the water, probing with my ski-stick. Slimy rocks against my feet. Stones rolling over my toes in the current. I had a mind to keep to the riverbed by shuffling but when about halfway and quite waist-deep my foot slipped into a hole. I went over backwards. In an action that seemed horribly slow I reached to stab my ski-pole and pushed and leant hard as if crowbarring something deep in the bed. I righted and tried a step. And another. Deeper but not much and I waded to the opposite bank and barefoot over snow to a small tree and laid out my mat and thumped life back into my feet.

I flailed my arms and yelled my line to Nick. He'd been watching and was ready. He crossed naked to the waist and bawled with relief at reaching my place by the tree. Another hour and it would have been too late.

Saplings of native trees had been planted some years before on the south bank and we picked through this dwarf wood and arrived at the open moor. Clouds drifting in from the west pulled a screen over the hills we'd seen earlier and our day turned grey. We angled over the pitted moor for the southeast quarter as if to climb Fionn Bheinn, but slunk south for a gap in the hills, a defile that promised a way to Loch a'Chroisg and Achnasheen. Before too long a path began to appear between drifts. It curved south and dropped towards the slit of a river, the crash of meltwater accompanying us on the twists and bends and finally to below the snowline and an old plantation of spruce. By degrees the path became a track though no vehicle had been on it for an age. We found out why. Further into the wood we were faced with upturned pines, one stacked upon another, their rootplates reared in tons of earth and stone and betraying a blunt force lately here. The Atlantic-born storm of early January had left this decades' old plantation strewn in new and disturbing arrangements. I thought the storm had been aided by the valley sides compressing the air into a vortex, this punching holes and the rearguard ransacking the core.

There were too many trunks to climb so we scurried down banks into the gloomy undergrowth and picked through the remaining groves. At the valley bottom we trundled along the lochside, then the banks of the river. We barely saw a car. In the dark I became entangled in some fallen tree limbs, torn more like. The same storm for sure. I sat on one of the branches and dug into my rucksac for my headtorch and threw a harsh electric light over the brash. Small cones on the ground. A litter of needles in faded copper. It was a larch.

We walked a way beyond Achnasheen to a wood for our parcel, a train clattering loosely on its slow climb to the village, a couple of lighted carriages disembodied in the wide dark of the moor. I imagined the idle warmth of passengers, the tea trolley, the guard reading the papers. A soft concussive of wheels over rail joists repeated over and fading into silence.

About a month back we'd made a food stash in the small wood and I struggled to remember exactly where. By a rotting log and covered over with moss and pine needles, I recalled. Close to a burn. Rotting logs and pine needles were plentiful but I found what I thought was the burn and tracked it up, pausing at likely places to poke the ground as if checking for snakes. There was something familiar about the arrangement of sticks. I called to Nick. His torchbeam came through the understory in odd flashes. When he came over we unearthed the tupperware box and a cache of tins. Nick inspected the contents.

'Bugger. There's only one gas. That won't be enough.'

'We'll get a fire going somewhere.'

'We'll have to. I can't live without tea. I don't fancy raw pasta. What's on the menu tonight?'

'Anything in a tin. Let's see.'

The tins were in a bin liner. I let them tumble out and laid them on the forest floor to read the labels.

'Lobster soup, haggis, new potatoes, fruit cocktail, cream.'

'Wow.'

The ground was pierced by tree roots and on a slope, and we were long in finding a spot for our tents. I gathered palmfuls of needles and made a thin mattress to smother the roots and lay down and was quite pleased. Nick made home on the slope above. I did the cooking by throwing tins together and afterwards Nick claimed it was the best meal he'd ever had. Well, for three days at least, he said.

We talked as I heated water for more tea. I told Nick about Fionn Bheinn, which climbs three thousand feet a little to the north. I'd been on this hill with Clive a few years before. I fleshed out the story because it was a good story, though not an unusual one. I never saw it as a premonition, some warning to heed. But it stoked a memory that our lives work to patterns that we could read. If we chose to.

It was the last week in March and springlike when we skirted Loch Fannich from the ruinous Nest and approached the watery footings of Fionn Bheinn. Frogspawn and a fresh green underfoot and below us light pooled on a small loch with a solitary island. The loch vanished as we reached the snowline. Cloud blew in and on the final ridge spindrift rattled our hoods. At the summit we lingered only long enough to fix a bearing. I led off, head bowed, Clive right behind. Falling snow masked our tracks almost as soon as they were made. I must have put in a spurt because when I turned Clive wasn't there. I waited some minutes then tried to retrace my steps but couldn't. My steps had gone and so had Clive's. He'd no map but there was only one way down from here. I'd see him at Achnasheen station, I thought. I headed off and had a while to wait for the train but when it arrived there was no Clive. As we pulled away I scanned the hillside for a small loping figure but no one on the sour pasture or among the burgundy of last year's bracken, the higher ground white and without feature, most of it lost to cloud. In Inverness I gave it two hours then phoned the police. I was convinced that after losing sight of me he'd strayed too far east and so had a long walk to the road and this I told them. They took details about his lack of map and compass and that he carried no phone.

'And you weren't worried?'

'Not really. I knew he'd appear, though with a story no doubt.'

'How were you so sure?'

'I just knew Clive.'

'So what happened?'

'I went out for meal with a couple of friends. Pre-arranged.'

'You're joking?'

'Why, what would you have done?'

'Probably rounded up those same friends and gone back out to look for him.'

'Well, all the talk about was about Clive and how we all needed to start a search.'

'Makes sense. What did you say?'

'I said yes, but let me finish my curry first.'

Nick shook his head.

'Then my phone rang.'

'Clive?'

'Who else?'

'The police. His family?'

'No, it was Clive calling from home. He sounded tired. He said he'd gone down the wrong way and had to walk a load of extra miles and got a lift back. Just as I'd thought. I heard his doorbell and he was gone a minute. When he came back he said it was the police. They needed a statement. It could take a while. So I left him to it.

Nick was supping his tea.

'Why didn't you call the police as soon as you got back?' he said.

'I was convinced he would turn up. He's always been slow coming down. But he can walk all day no problem. He had tremendous stamina. I just knew in my gut nothing serious had happened. What was I to do? Phone his parents? They would have been frantic. It would have wrecked their evening.'

'And it didn't ruin yours?'

'I knew Clive would show with some great tale. And he did. Years before he'd lost contact with a friend on a hill in Glencoe and his friend immediately reported him missing. On a hot summer's day as well. When he got to his car he found the police there, his friend giving a statement.'

'A tad embarrassing.'

'You could say that. He was furious.'

Nick said he was going to turn in and listen to a lecture. Bedtime story for him. I lay on my side and read but I wasn't reading. I couldn't erase the thought of Clive up there in the snow lost and searching for my footprints. I knew he didn't carry much gear and usually relied on me for a map. When someone said my attitude was blasé I shrugged. You don't know Clive, I said. He doesn't fit the mould. I never heard him say I'd abandoned him. Clive never thought much of it, just another tale for the pub and bothy.

I held my book up to the light. What had I just read? I flicked back the pages until I found a familiar line but the words swam. I wasn't just thinking about Clive being lost up there but something else. The fallen larch by the river.

A stand of larch on a quiet section of the River Nairn not a mile from my home were at least a century old, overhanging the waters and perhaps planted there to give shade for salmon in spawning time. That day as usual I'd gone downriver with Hollie beyond the larches, an especially raw day towards the end of March, Hollie sniffing about the odd blooming periwinkle and harsh white of snowdrops. A false herald. The yellow blooms of the gorse were firmly closed, as were the celandines and aconites. Last season's vegetation had a shelled-out appearance, pale or dun in colour. Dead grass blew about in the wind, a wind that had blown almost continuously from the east for three weeks and over the weekend had reached a crescendo, the gale tearing through the river woods and dumping brash over the path and half-wrenching from a beech a great limb that now hung creaking as if to keep time. I was on my way back and had reached the larches when I fielded a call on my mobile. The police. When I confirmed my name the voice told me that Clive had not appeared for work. He said he'd had been out on a walk somewhere and did I have any notion of where he might have gone? They would come around for a statement. When I came down the lane a police-car and two officers were waiting. Just at that moment Anne arrived from work, her face all concern. Anne made tea while I answered questions, simple framing ones first – last seen, last message, had he spoken about a walk, where did he like to go? I checked my phone. His last text was three or four days ago. A walk? He'd not said. I'd planned to go skiing, cancelled due to the wind. Everything had been cancelled. The forecasted storm had duly arrived, a dry continental blast that reached a hundred miles an hour in the Cairngorms and gave southwest Scotland and Cumbria their worst snow in thirty years. Like everyone else I'd battened down for the weekend. They scribbled. I searched my memory of the last time I saw and spoke with Clive, in his flat over a pot of tea. I tried to conjure the atmosphere, the small details that were suddenly important. What equipment might he have taken? We can find out, I said and we drove to his flat in Inverness where he'd lived for fifteen years and forced the door. Just how I remembered it from two weeks before, untidy but homely, the piles of clothes and loose documents. On the hallway wall a large pinboard with photos of his life, holidays, countries he'd visited, house parties and groups of friends and plenty with him in the hills. A book by his bed, *How to Write Sitcoms*. His grey waterproof jacket was gone but everything else there, ice-axe, crampons, overnight gear, all in his storeroom. I looked around. The worn furnishings humanshaped by their usage and every corner and cranny breathing out friendliness. There was little thought and no design to any of it yet it spoke so strongly of one person and of his immediate presence, as if he'd just popped out to the shops. How exteriors can lie, when events unknowable have already moved on. I gazed from the window to the roundabout, one of the busiest in the city. I once stayed for some weeks and remember the constant drone of traffic but it never seemed to bother him, however much he loved the peace of the hills.

His blue waterbottle that he always took lay empty and unscrewed on the fridge. I wondered what that meant. If he'd planned a walk it was to be a short one and perhaps that narrowed it but when later the police requested I make a list of places Clive might have gone I realised it wasn't so easy. He might have gone anywhere.

There were voices in the night and I thought at first I was dreaming. A car parked in the layby perhaps a quarter mile away, its headlights through a wickerwork of trees. A man and woman arguing. Neither was listening to the other, their voices rising and overlapping then a short momentary silence and more shouting, the private disquiet of their lives spilling over the wild country and under stars that had begun to appear and I couldn't help but think it compromised the peace here. I wondered why they had chosen the loneliest layby on all the road to have their row. So none other could hear and no third testimony be logged? But I also thought, could the hurt spoken ever be undone or was the final word some quantum tipping point and their paths now forever divided? A slamming of doors, the engine revving and fading into the night.

The dawn light was a late show, struggling to breach the canopy, and we decamped in gloom, Nick was slow. He showed me his foot.

'How does it feel?' I said.

'Swollen.'

'Is it sore?'

'A little.'

'I have some pills, in fact I've plenty.' I lobbed over the packet.

'You know I won't use them.'

'Have them anyway.'

He tucked them into one of his pouches and stood up and followed as I bent under branches and tried to remember the way out. Nick's feet aside, as the thaw continued my main concern was river crossings. South from here lay a large empty quarter, hills and lochs arranged by geology in east-west alignments so our route was by passes and the fording of rivers. All these rivers were born of great snow-holding corries and all were running high. Even without climbing to the summits it would be four days before we reached a road and only a roadhead at that.

By a cleated footbridge we crossed the River Carron and on duckboards crossed the marshy valley flats to a shuttered cottage. A Scottish Rights of Way trail led under the railway and into an enclosure of young trees, Scots pine mostly, planted at random and a few already ten-foot and rocking in the strong breeze. Soon we began to encounter large drifts, the snow piled to uncertain depths, thawing and hazardous, and as we gained height towards the watershed the cover became general. Now facing into a steady wind we stopped to unfold the wet tents and spread them and tied the guys to rocks so they lolled about like great flags. In the shelter of our rucksacs I warmed soup and studied the map. The old path connected the two glens of Carron and Conon but we were heading west and so would leave it and come to the valley of the Meig by a wilder route. I scanned the ground ahead, the mountains clad in grey raincoats, their steep and broken footings running east to west and below this a path, from here just a pencil line but tortuous through the scree and past a grey ruin and vanishing upcountry.

With the tents stowed away I led us on a slow descent reckoned fair by sight though in fact it was fraught and drawn-out. Hollows and ditches and all burn channels were snow-filled as were unseen folds and the rear of every bank, the ongoing thaw rendering it all soft and baseless. Surfaces were hard to judge and we trod the soft fields in a state of anxiety. Where we could we linked bare ground and from high on a shoulder looked down onto the valley of the Meig. Left was the upper reaches of Strathconon, heather and conifers and the sheen of Loch Beannacharain. Parcelled tight by Scardroy Lodge was a field-enriched pasture. I was struck by it. The winter scene framed like an old daguerreotype but hand-tinted in its centre. The colour of jade. Drizzle was followed by sunshine and a great rainbow, the gullied slopes across the valley shaded and the birchwoods stencilled and brassy against the scree.

The Meig rose in pitch as we neared. Ground that a day or two ago had lain under a foot of snow now squelched with melt and the river itself a gathering torrent, a thing of churn and jostle. We turned upstream to trace its valley and search for a safe point to ford. The day was mild again and the river rising and I felt we needed to cross soon. Twice where it braided and seemed shallow enough I stopped and talked to Nick and pointed to a line linking the shoals, but he wouldn't entertain it, not here. He said the river's speed was such it could take your legs away like a rugby tackle, and even if you were able to swim in such cold you would struggle to regain the bank. What if you became separated from your rucksac, he said. I pictured that in my head. He was right. We went on.

In one section floods had torn off a length of bank and raised it and left it aground like some enormous pike. There were gravel deposits and those of sand and the trunk of a mountain ash stripped of bark and much bludgeoned. On a great meander the river went broadly over some falls, these formed by shelves of rock that intersected our way in a prominent step as if fashioned as a crude boundary to mark something. Once a portal to the last land of meso tribes with its wildwoods and wolves.

If the river flats seemed heavily grazed the craggy slopes on either side held remnants of the old woods, a sign perhaps that deer had not routed this estate as they had others. In another mile the river was broader. It still lacked shoals or stones breaking the surface but I reasoned it might just be shallow enough to be safe. Nick seemed happy. We undressed to the waist. I went in and the waters reached only to my thighs but the weight and press of it was unsettling. I reached the gravel on the far bank, turned and shouted. Nick was sitting on his rucksac bare-legged. He raised a walking pole in a lazy acknowledgment, his face all but expressionless. He crossed easily.

On a wedge of land where the Allt an Amise ran from a pass to the south and joined the Meig I scraped a space in the shrinking snowcover and pitched, Nick as usual just flattened the snow and bored in his pegs. Crisscrossing the surface was the spoor of beasts, numerous deer and pawprints belonging to a cat or fox. They mirrored the river's course for some yards then went off on vectors and I followed one to behind some rocks. The carcass of a deer not long dead and without a mark, though it had probably lain buried for days. As it was downriver from where we'd collected water I wasn't concerned.

To save fuel I cooked a common meal of pasta and to this added fish, tomato, fresh onion. I was hungry. When ready I went to lift the pan and managed to knock it over. Nick wondered about the swearing. I spooned it back, rewarmed it, and when I handed him his share it contained flecks of last year's grass, dried strings of cellulose like a type of worm that seemed to come alive when stirred. He looked at it absently, took it away and said it was good.

The snow that had put such a brake on our progress was largely gone by morning, if only in the valley. One thought as I dismantled was that maybe the snow's softness had in fact been a friend to Nick's feet, a great mattress to cushion his footfalls. We'd walked on it almost continuously since the schoolhouse at Duag some ten days ago. It was only a thought and I didn't ask and when I'd finished packing I sat and half-watched Nick in his rituals. The second his last pannier was stuffed and strapped I swung for the path that climbed south, the only line of weakness in the barrier of hills guarding the empty reaches of Monar and Strathfarrar.

There was something rust-coloured by the burn. Yesterday's carcass had been opened and gorged upon in the dark, by a fox or some carnivorous bird or maybe both. A coarse butchery it appeared and not surprising given how these creatures survive, but they'd removed the rich vital organs and viscera first and all will go before it can rot, nothing wasted in this hungry country, not even bones that one day will lime the ground and raise calcareous plants in an otherwise acid land. The sour soil spoke largely of its geology and as we gained height old gravel beds from old floods were now overrun with leafless blaeberry and moss grew thick on stumps betraying a time when trees were plentiful here.

Bloated by melt the burn increasingly emerged from tunnels in the drifts that crossed and re-crossed our path, and in time water and path disappeared under a general covering and we navigated as best we could. West the land rose to Maolie Lunndaidh, its broad crown lost in a cloud cap that had dogged us since the Fannichs. We paused, hoping the clouds would lift but they didn't and we climbed on to the pass and over it and into the lands of Monarside, a segment of loch now visible in the valley below. On this side a great quantity of snow extended for a mile at least along Coire Rionnarach, softening with the day and although we crossed the expanse with vigilance I went through twice to some cavity and the second time wrenched a knee and hobbled afterwards. A group of skinny-looking deer trotted away. When at a good distance they stopped and watched us pass. Other groups were about and none seemed to be feeding on the thin sward. The vegetation in this glen appeared so denuded that even amongst the crags there lived barely a tree. Over the years I'd noted the barrenness prevalent here and if anything it had become worse.

Towards the loch and below the snowline the river gained greatly in volume. If I considered it might be an idea to cross while we could, I didn't say. We stuck to the path and the river remained on our right and uncrossed. There was a time in the last century when all the waters in this valley arrived at Loch Monar via a delta, an almost level fan of deposits built up over millennia that told the story of the loch's hydrology since the last Ice Age and of which old surveys of this region bore witness. In fact before the building of the dam in 1960 Loch Monar possessed many such features. On early maps they are marked as small growths at the mouths of rivers, low-lying and almost flat and barely above the original height of the waters and in reality a place of silt and marsh and washed over by seasonal floods. A special habitat for birds and for types of birds that were only found by such inland features. Of these deltas the largest was formed by the waters leaving Coire Rionnarach, and the last people to see it said it stretched hundreds of yards into the loch, a place familiar to the Gael for thousands of years even if the name is lost. The dam raised the water-level by just one hundred and fifty feet but enough to double the loch's length and refigure entirely its shoreline. The deltas are gone. The birds are gone. The waters now reach a mile further up the corrie, a great indent that divides the path at this point, we taking the one west.

The main river we crossed using an estate bridge but the path dissipated and before us was another sizable burn and one that drained the south-facing corries of Maolie Lunndaidh. In no mood for a delay I opted for a line of submerged boulders and jumped rock to rock and reached the bank shouting and gesturing to Nick. Easy, I said. Nick looked across the rapids for some time. He sat and removed his boots and went to wade the deeper sections. The waters rode a good bit over his knees and he jabbed each pole ahead and shuffled for fear of losing his footing, like someone dragging the river.

We climbed to a shoulder and in stages dropped to the loch, what remaining of the path running alongside it. Despite the wet autumn the loch was ringed by the scar of drawdown where nothing grew and nothing could grow as the soil has long since gone, eroded away by the drastic and controlled ebb and flow of waters. A steady west wind ran at us unhindered and with it strings of cold drizzle and the hills ahead all curtained in grey.

When Nick caught me up I asked about his feet. Fine, he said, which was what he always said. When I suggested we camp he said we'd better keep going, what with the snow being so slow and crossing that river. Okay, I said, let's get to Thomson's old place and see how we are.

In less than an hour we came across a grove of mature Scots pine that broke the starkness of their surroundings. I knew the trees were planted a century ago and familiar to Iain Thomson, a shepherd and keeper here in the late 1950s and last person to live on this side of the loch before the dam. The pines are the topmost survivors of a small wooded area that nestled about the keeper's croft and Strathmore Lodge, a place of birdsong and haunt of many a creature. All now lie beneath the steely waters.

Here was shelter but with an hour left of daylight and the promise of a big climb tomorrow we agreed to push on. A burn coming from the hanging corrie above was a scarf of white on the hillside, Where it reached the wood it divided and ran by channels among a fall of boulders. A few weatherbeaten planks spanning the worst section was all the bridge there was and for the other channels I climbed upriver and went from island to island and crossed them by turn. Nick was behind and I watched him drop so I could see only the crown of his hat. Then I heard a shout. I went back and found him grief-stricken. He'd lost one of his walking poles. Just wrenched from his grip, he said, as if by something alive in the water. He was on the far bank but we could communicate by shouting. I began to wander the burn on my side scanning likely pools. Downstream it cut a great trench beneath the pines and below this it surged and pooled among large boulders and ran into the loch maybe two hundred yards away. At no point did its speed let up. I believed his missing pole to be out there in the loch and gone but I searched nonetheless. Nick was higher up and when he looked down on me I shrugged and shook my head. I went a little lower and found the stick trapped in an eddy, the bucket end pointing skywards and turning like a strange periscope.

A pulse of rain blew in from the loch. A mile across the waters a light blinked on, then another, the year-round inhabitants of Pait Lodge conceding to the midwinter gloom. When Nick crossed over we looked about for somewhere to camp.

One of the trees had been freshly toppled, its great rootball squared to the west like some barricade and its canopy broken into brash. It was hard to conceive the kind of freak gust that had done this, unhinged such a tree, a specimen that had withstood a hundred prior winters and every recorded storm. A dead stag there as well. Fully antlered, its neck horribly twisted and face set in terror as if it had died of fright. It may have been blown down the bank like the tree or just perished in the blizzard and maybe in that order.

The bank gave shelter but as I didn't fancy a night so close to the poor creature we went a little downstream and pitched on sloping and rough ground, barely fit for a tent. In the last light and with empty rucksacs we scouted the mouth of the burn for firewood and found plenty. Roots and stumps from an interglacial forest loosened by shore waves and floated to various high waters or come down in spates and lying in every attitude, the final traces of an old tree cover. We broke to length those pieces we could and tied up the rest and hauled our bundles to a rock table close to the burn and made a small fire, a light here now like the one across the loch. The flames sawed wildly and sparks died in the blackness and we were doused in resin-smoke no matter where we sat. Nick raked the embers and rested his pot by the coals and boiled water. Noodles followed by tea. Taste of smoke. He sipped and pursed his lips and said, you could pay good money for this.

'What,' I said, 'smoky tea or a fire in the hills?'

'Probably both. Smoky tea is all the rage. But our love of hills is odd don't you think?'

'Why so? It comes pretty naturally to me.'

'Well, for thousands of years folk in search of game have wandered here and made camp and moved on and sat by fires like this, but they'd done it from necessity and not because they'd had a free weekend and fancied a few Munros.'

'Not like us you mean?'

'Don't kid yourself. Our journey is a distraction. We shape it into something gallant, some notion that feeds our soul but really there's no need for us to be here.'

Nick blew into his mug.

'I do wonder though about those people,' he said, 'our early forebears who passed through here after the ice and hung on until the settled culture of herders and farmers. They left no records beyond artefacts. Did the hills frighten them in the same way they frightened farmers and town dwellers of later centuries?'

'I don't see how they did,' I said. 'Those guys hunted and foraged. They depended on the hills and woods for their survival. It provided everything. We used to believe these early peoples were primitive and even barbaric but in fact the opposite is the case. There's no question early hunters were responsible for the decline and probable extinction of great beasts, so-called megafauna like mammoths and great elk, but in general they trod lightly, perhaps because there were relatively few of them. Their relationship with nature was way more harmonious than ours, and the fragments of that culture surviving today, in Central Africa, the Amazon and even the Arctic are testimony to that.'

'So you think we became fearful?'

'I do. You could say it emerged from the need to protect cropland and domestic animals from predators, a matter of life and death for early farmers, but from that fear came the desire to subjugate, or so the argument goes.'

'That's lazy thinking to my mind. Our recent ancestors didn't slaughter millions of bison because they were seen as a threat. It was simple exploitation, taking something that appears abundant and free. And it continues today at a relentless pace.'

Nick took his mug and drained it and wiped his mouth with the back of his hand.

'I'm talking about the economic imperative,' he said. 'Forget the idea that deep in our human psyche exists some innate need to control our environment. Most of us love nature, find joy in it, and I'm not surprised given we spent two million years pretty much wedded to it, as you said. But there are now economists who are coining the idea that all nature has a monetary value and its protection or otherwise depends on some calculation of its worth to us, now or in the future.'

'The commodification of nature. Ecosystem services. Give everything a price, even a lump of rock. So it can be measured. It's a reductionist way of looking at things, but where does that leave butterflies?'

'Meaning?'

'I mean how do you weigh the worth of such a beautiful winged creature?'

'You can't. As a means of saving the planet the idea of pricing nature is deeply flawed but it stems from our drive for economic growth, of treating the world as a bottomless pit of treasure.'

Nick poked at the one the roots. A shower of sparks ran with the smoke and died in the dark.

'Not sure what the answer is,' he said. 'People want stuff.'

'Yes they do, we do. We're all complicit. Outdoor kit for instance. Your jacket wasn't cheap. We could change the world tomorrow but we choose not to and instead we blame poor countries for their mushrooming populations and how they treat their own environment. China pours its sewage into the Yellow Sea but we still want their cheap goods. The poor aren't going to take lessons from the rich. Look at how we've screwed up our own patch. Look at this place.'

'This estate?'

'Yes, look at how it's managed. Maybe mismanaged is more the word.'

'Or neglected.'

'Neglect would be good.'

'How come?'

'Well, consider how we control the deer population. At present Highland estates cull their quota of deer and in doing so merely maintain numbers at a high level, a level that prevents trees from regenerating naturally.'

'So they need to cull more.'

'Yes they do, and that would be the sensible thing, but most private estates won't. Not in their interests.'

'Neglect would be even worse, surely,' Nick said. 'If the estates stopped even their limited cull, deer numbers would multiply.'

'They would, for a time. Then when the grazing ran out the population would crash. It's nature's way. Happens to other species in the wild.'

'You think the trees would return?'

'Yes, eventually. Even without an apex predator. You might get rhododendron and knotweed by loch shores but native trees and introduced exotics would outmuscle all and provide for diverse habitats. If humans entirely vacated the Highlands, fenced it off and left it for a century entire forests would re-establish and with it a broad array of wildlife. Nature tends towards abundance.'

'Leave it for a hundred years? I don't know. It would be easier just to bring back the wolf. A few roaming packs would change everything.'

Nick opened his palms to the blaze and turned them and turned them back. He talked of how his studies related to these issues, of how scientists have shifted in their understanding of ecosystems, believing now that they largely work from the top down, the so-called 'trophic cascades'. Top predators indirectly benefit plants and lower life forms by controlling meso-predators and herbivores. He cited examples. The removal of wolves from most northern American states has resulted in an explosion of coyote numbers whose impact and control is now costing hundreds of millions of dollars. When wolves were reintroduced into Yellowstone after a seventy-five year absence they prevented overgrazing by elk. Willow began to grow along riverbanks again, their shade cooling the water temperatures for trout which in turn fostered a return of the beaver whose pools provided a home for amphibians and small birds. He said one of the most studied effects of apex predator removal was the hunting of sea otters almost to extinction in the nineteenth century off the Aleutian Islands. This caused sea urchins to multiply which then stripped kelp beds to sandy wastes. Their protection and an increase in numbers of sea otters have seen a return of the beds. But worldwide the picture is bleak. The extirpation of top predators is creating a sickness and vacuum in the web of life that will affect us all.

I nodded and as if to move the conversation on spoke of the dam and how it had transformed these surroundings. Before 1960 Thomson's cottage marked the furthest west of the loch and beyond this was some four miles of alluvial flats where the Abhainn an t-Sratha meandered, a place prone to small inundations and known for its thousands of waders and waterfowl which nested there every spring, teals, dunlin, snipes, greenshanks, mallards, scooter swans. Thomson delighted in their calling and ornithologists have noted it was one the finest places in mainland Britain to witness such a display.

I looked over to the dark water and even darker hills, black like a coalface in their profiles drawn against the great lid of cloud. The lights of Pait across the water and I wondered what they made of our fire as fires are now seldom here. Maybe the last of note were piles of burning brash when the woods were felled for the dam, Thomson's cottage also, flaming like a beacon and great pillows of smoke streaming lochwards in the rain-shadow. When the great wall at Monar was finished the waters rose with surprising rapidity. Fathoms where there was once Highland air and in three months all trace of croft and lodge were gone. The river flats as well and the pinewoods of Reidh Cruaidh and countless shoreline features thousands of years in the making and all of it irreplaceable. A flooding to foreshadow an inundation on much greater scale and maybe then the small vanities will go, this wall and others brick by brick removed and valleys restored and land recolonised with creatures that call and cry again over vagrant camps such as ours.

After supper we drank more tea and Nick built up the fire in a hail of embers. The glowing coals warmed but a wind from the heights sent a chill to our backs. I stepped away and climbed the bank. Nick down there by the fire, a small ring of light in the encompassing dark, transitory and the only thing it conjured was that tomorrow there would be dark here again. I said I was going to my tent and by torchlight sought the domed flysheet and downy warmth of my bag. The noise from the burn was almost too much at first but lying there I began to tune it out, or rather the sound withdrew, something there yet not intruding.

I slept and dreamt what I'd dreamt many times, a witness to events, a corroboration of the outcome. Armed with a premonition I'd gone to his flat on that bright and wild morning to caution but he would not listen and so I went with him west along the narrow road, gusts in the valley making the car lurch like a fairground ride. In such wind Clive had no ambition for the coast path. One section is chiselled from a bluff above shore-rocks and kelp, a deathtrap in such winds. Instead he crossed the bridge to the mixed wood and with the trees leaning and creaking he climbed the path out and up the hill flank. A fight with the wind but rewarded with a view to the great crooked arm of the loch and raw hills beyond so arrayed they might have been carved by a race of demonic quarrymen. The winter cold had silenced the seeps and high running waters, a sparkle of petrified ice up there among the brunet heathers and grasses and to one of these he climbed, there to marvel at what the cold had created. I was there with him and I wasn't. I saw the mechanical inevitability, the cogs in motion and wheels in their trunnions and a metronome marking the passing seconds, the minutes, the last uphill steps on a path with no turning. Of this I was a ghost and a dumb witness.

Eight

There were no stars, the night so black I could see nothing and all night I heard a soughing wind and sometimes drizzle on the flysheet and the burn muttering. I shouted over to Nick when it was still dark and later I opened the vestibule to a deep crimson sky framing the hills in the east. This faded and a clag set in long before we'd decamped and were afoot westwards by the loch. The pale and stirring waters carrying a sky heavy with impending rain. Of the hills ahead only their foundations were visible, their upper slopes missing as if sheared off so their true heights could only be guessed at. The country had a ransacked appearance, winter herbage a pale green and all was cropped down to its roots and if mosses were palatable to the grazers they would be gone too. Close to our narrow path were the remains of some animal, just the shoulder-blade it seemed and bleached by the weathers. I looked at it, puzzled. It appeared to belong to no creature of these parts and I wondered if it had recently lain buried and been unearthed by some spate or even by rabbits. Some part of a beast now extinct. Whose epoch was brief and to this day not recorded.

The loch at this west end sat so shallow its surface was marked by small islands of rubble, each like a fallen cairn, old markers on a forgotten map. The path segmented then faded as we knew it would, access to these wild parts easier by boat though oddly as we approached the loch's muddy terminus there were traces of the old pre-dam way used by Thomson and others. The map said it swung north towards Bealach Cruhain but it goes nowhere in particular and the land is largely without track. We forded the burn draining Coille Tollie Chaorachain and began to enter the sanctuary from which a ring of peaks soared three thousand feet. Our only way through was a high saddle between the summits of Bidein a' Choire Sheasgaich and Lurg Mhor.

Two rivers flow into the loch at its mouth and with a big ascent to come we paused at the first for some soup. Nick cradled his mug and gazed up at what of our route could be seen, the land rising to a corrie of snow and a headwall that propped the upper mountain, all glimpsed beneath a frayed base of clouds. It looked a long way, he said.

I crossed at this point. Nick skirted the bank and crossed where it narrowed and offered the aid of boulders. The second river was too deep so we traced its course through increasingly broken and rock-strewn ground. On the steeper slopes were pockets of refugia, stands of birch and in the crannies of a ravine dwarf sorbus, wind-bent and sheathed in moss. Here the river dog-legged, and we crossed by jumping to a stone midflow and gathered ourselves before a final leap, the waters sluicing and pouring sheer into a pool twenty feet below. By hands we climbed a steep grassy bank and picked through outcroppings and sometimes over them, the land lifting to a kind of lip and beyond this dark rockbands slashed by three waterfalls, each issuing from drifts of hanging snow, the meltwater in one running straight and foaming along some faultline as if engineered to do so.

I thought I'd miscalculated and maybe we'd begun our climb too soon. My neck ached from staring upwards. I knew these hills well but had never approached from the loch and there's no sensible reason why you might. A lower pass lay to the north, a steady rise of land pillowed in great drifts, the col itself hidden by mist. Easier and a good deal safer but it would add miles and hours to the day and so wasn't an option.

Keeping the burn on our right we went hand over hand up a snowless outcrop and into the upper corrie, the slope easing at first to a great snow-bowl and this framed by blueish cliffs and the blurred edge of cloud. On firmer snow and with ice axes and many halts we climbed the best part of an hour. The halts gave me time to judge broadly the arrangement of features in relation to our travel. I began to veer west though in reality the looming blocks of cliff-face corralled us that way regardless.

At some point I made out a crescent of clean snow against the pale of moving cloud. The summit of the pass, the greater part of it bulging with a cornice. We gathered at some rocks. I pointed the line we should take, aslant of the fall line and less steep than a direct approach. I said we should go one at a time, me to cut simple steps and he to follow. Well, don't slip, Nick said, and he nodded and appeared almost happy, a wry grin on his face. He had a steady head for such a situation and now seemed lost in the moment, a kind of absorption that purged briefly the clutter that so weighed him down. I looked at the sweep of slope below and went slowly up, a step, a swing of the axe. I fell into an easy rhythm. I reached the crest in a howling westerly and crouched and waved a gloved hand and watched Nick stitch his steps to mine, slow, precise, a dark loping figure against the empty snow.

When he came over the crest I'd already set the compass. A thousand feet of snow to descend then a sodden hillside until Loch Calavie shaped itself from the mist and rose to meet us. A dark mile of it and all but free of ice.

At a ribbon of snow along its shoreline I waited. High winds ran the mist streaming from An Riabhachan and its great neighbour Sgurr na Lapaich, and in the gaps of sky beyond were ruddy reefs of cloud. By some quirk the basin to the southwest held a strange brightness, bog-pools holding the sky and grasses like a pale rash over the heather, their dead blades flattened where snow had recently lain. The signs were misleading for the valley began to darken and as we halted to examine the river egressing the loch for a safe fording point I knew we were fast losing the day.

The river was the first barrier to our crossing of the Ling Basin, a wild morass of ditches and pools, and with a bothy at its southern fringe. I judged the flow too fast so we swung back east and hoped by doing so we would find easier ground but didn't. There is no obvious way to thread the two miles of watery peatland and as the light faded our options narrowed. We retraced our way to the river and crossed by stripping and wading and the time it took were the last minutes of salvageable light. The River Ling a mile further on was wider and deeper but I thought if we could strike its bank at a point where it ran into Loch Cruoshie then at least its flow might be less.

In fact when we stood on its bank after a struggle with our torches the current was so slow it barely gave off a sound. I ran my torchbeam over the surface and I went in bare to the waist, my feet over a silty mud and waters lapping around my groin before I was even midway. The muddy bed seemed almost without foundation. A few more steps and I began to sink. I lifted a foot, shifted balance, rocked unsteadily. Another step and I would be over and floating to the open space of Loch Cruoshie. Nick was sitting on his rucksac watching. I climbed back onto the bank.

'No?'

'No chance.'

'We could camp here'.

'What if it rains? The hills are still loaded with snow. We'd be trapped.'

'Ok, so how far up this river will we need to go?'

'I don't know.'

I walked barefoot with my boots yoked about a shoulder and we scouted the bank and twice tried to cross and twice failed so I pulled on my socks and footwear and went on for most of the next hour, we now moving directly away from the bothy. Our torchlight was often over the water and when stones began to disrupt the flow we stepped into it for a fourth time. It was deep but we made the crossing.

In my unsteady light the path on the far bank was a string of silver and I knew there was just a single wet mile to a refuge that once stood as the loneliest house in mainland Britain, at least in terms of neighbours. Coming here over the years had given it a strong familiarity but a general one and at the day's death came details now remembered, the groove of path over extruded bedrock, wigs of moss and a hydrology that has channels leaning south and none ever obliged your travel. The footings of a shieling more covered year by year. Rusting ironwork of a boundary fence. At the last corner I waited for Nick's light to crest the rise and when it did I moved on until just ahead the land banked, and stamped dark against the starless night was a gable end. The bothy. Inside it was so cold at first it seemed little improvement, a dry place to pass the night and no more. I went out to fill my bottle and stood by the door and looked for Nick's bobbing torch. A detached thing floating there in the dark. I knew its every rise and fall and sideways drift and it spoke of the man and a mimic of the land itself, the light charting a template of the way lately trod. My own light I kept switched off.

I've seen the burn by the bothy frozen and once had to dig through a great drift to reach it, but I've never seen it dry, despite visiting during the height of a drought. Today it ran with its usual strength. The play of its waters carried through to the bothy and I wondered if it was a sound you ever got used to. If you were born to it could it carry you through life? I thought of the family of twelve living here more than a century ago, all in this one small space. I've known crowded bothies with their noise and clutter and all those cook stoves going at once and barely floorspace to stretch and sleep and barely any sleep for snoring. Quite different if you grew up in this throng and were nurtured in this wild place. I tried to imagine how such an experience might shape you. No human neighbours, everything coming in on the back of a pony, a realm only of moor and loch and wild creatures and bordered by a sightline of hill-crests and summits. Sound of water and birdsong and the love of a close-knit family. They stayed here in the last years before telegraph and radio and when cut off by winter snows or flooded rivers were as isolated as the lighthouse keepers out in the Atlantic. Formal schooling only happened when a teacher who travelled croft to croft came to stay, though there were enough little ones anyway to fill half a classroom, all ages, all abilities. A community in miniature, where everyone did their share and a mutual support prevailed over any disposition to selfishness. A hard life as they say and you would need to be resilient to come through it.

The Ling watershed is dotted with marks of past habitation but these were mostly ruinous by the time the shepherding couple moved here. A century ago their closest neighbours were over the pass at Iron Lodge or Pait at Monarside, both a five or six mile walk away, perhaps two hours in a pair of tackety boots. You might wonder how the barrier of hills shaped their outlook. Thomson mentions meeting one of the children, then a man in his seventies. The man asked Thomson to take him to the end of the loch where he might for a last time look upon the backdrop of his childhood. A short while afterwards Thomson read of his passing. Renwick his name, a Professor of Theology and sometime Moderator of the Free Church of Scotland.

I turned on the hard bunk and listened to the burn and thought of a suburban garden. Playing with my brothers, the hose on a hot day, lying on the grass amongst the drone and buzz of insects, all manner of flying things in the small sky. I never thought of the garden as a haven of wildness though looking back it obviously was. An ant's nest in the compost and ear-wigs and woodlice under every stone. Great spiders spun traps among the roses and stagbeetles roamed the lawn and from time to time hedgehogs slept in the shade beneath the mahonia. Our garden was bordered by dense shrubbery, and between this and the fence ran a secret crawling pathway, a corridor in the under-growth that I'd discovered or perhaps made. By stooping among dead-nettle and rhododendron you could travel the length of our plot without being seen. From this green tunnel I burrowed into our neighbour's garden and dodged five or six bad-tempered Pekinese to reclaim footballs, trespassing on a foreign land, but mostly I'd travel hands and knees the garden's length to a raised bank. Just because I could. A cross-hatched fence here looked onto some municipal tennis courts, rarely used. The bank was overhung by a Bramley apple tree and in autumn great sour and wormy cookers lay uncollected on the ground. I once gathered a barrowful of these giants and had my brother bowl them at me, I swatting them high over the fence and onto the courts. A great shower of broken apple making a pleasing mess, or an early judgement on concrete.

My childhood was maybe not so different. Save for the boundaries. I would happily have swapped a fear of traffic and trespass for that of a rising river or storm. I envied them their vast acreage, their freedom.

The bothy is sited on a raised terrace and at one time there was a neighbouring building here. Its tumbled walls had been fenced off and the small enclosure planted with native species of rowan, birch and pine. I happened to be staying here twenty years ago when two men were undertaking the task and I remember at the time thinking this must be the start of something, an embryo of a future wood that one day would cover the watershed and valley and send tentacles of fuzzy green up every burn. A foolish thought. It's true the trees have grown to twice my height and flourished in their cocoon but they remain stunted in range and wholly caged lest the deer strip their bark and eat their seedings. They exist as curios, museum pieces from another time. They speak of an estate which tends a garden of exotics for visitors by the road yet allows the interior to degrade. Whose vision is for poured concrete and little else. A fence is the feeble answer to the overstocking of deer and has no place in the wild Highlands. Fences inhibit the natural movement of creatures and create an artificial lushness within. If we can't protect our remaining woods without enclosing them then let's not bother.

When I went out barefoot to look at the trees I had to step around four dead hinds. One had been butchered and all looked emaciated and all with their eyes open. From the evidence of dung on the frosted turf a sizable herd had sheltered here.

Nick was still not up. I called again through the ceiling. A tired reply and the clop of feet on the rafters. He eventually came down the wooden stairs and entered the room, dishevelled, mouth agape. He paced the floor. Did he know the time? No. He said his feet had proved especially sore over the last miles and with that he drifted through the door and outside to soak them in the freezing burn.

When he reappeared I didn't chivvy him immediately into sorting his gear. I knew he wanted a break but I also knew we'd virtually no food and couldn't stay. Our next parcel was close to the mouth of the River Ling, a day's walk. If we wanted to eat tonight we needed to reach it. My right knee had puffed up after being caught in a snowdrift once too often and I put crushed snow in an empty food bag and clamped it around the swelling. I took some pills and gave a few to Nick who was by now swallowing them.

The room was festooned with dangling gear, on hooks and nails, draped over some cord and the back of the bench. As if the floorboards held some contaminant harmful to fabrics. In addition to the bench there was a sleeping platform and small table. I'd heard the wood for such furnishings had been carried in on the shoulders of volunteers five miles over the pass and that there had been many such loads. On the facing wall a framed photo of the surrounding hills, a dark study in monochrome which had been there for years. It had been taken one Hogmanay. I wondered which. There wasn't a scrap of snow anywhere in the image.

The other room where we'd hung the tents was empty of furnishings. A ground of flagstones, a hearth, a few blunt saws on rusty nails. No fuel and none to gather, the land around long since looted of trees. There used to be a friendly note encouraging folk to cut peat and a nearby bank was opened to facilitate this but it didn't catch on. Too few visitors and those few after rough miles and river crossings too tired to cut and haul back a sackload of peat, peat for future visitors at that.

Nick's treasured bag of coconut milk powder had split and its contents all but gone. A tired discovery of last night and he now seemed stoical about the loss and shook what he could over his porridge, a small white cloud rising above his bowl. I sat and read and said nothing. Nick worked slowly and with an air of woe. He paced and gathered his items and assigned them to small piles on the table. I thought maybe the burst packet had knocked him though probably he was just overtired and his feet ached. I didn't ask. Apart from Nick's mutterings and a vague fall of water the silence was palpable. He picked up a food packet and studied the label and said something I couldn't quite catch, a moan of annoyance, and he looked up as if to appeal to someone in the roof joists, some masked figure with strings who might have a say over the arrangement on the table. When we left to begin our journey down the Ling it was almost noon and I was beside myself with frustration.

Yesterday's peaks were still hidden but the cloudbase had risen to reveal snow reaching down in great corrugations. In this sallow light we fixed ourselves on the left bank of the Ling, the chief conduit draining the basin and whose headwaters were a tiny lochain close by the summit of Aonach Buidhe, a great hill to our south. I'd hoped the overnight freeze might have calmed the flow but it hurried past and I was glad we had no reason to cross over and could keep to this side for its entire course, a dozen miles or so to its mouth at Loch Long. I knew the upper valley to be pathless and notoriously rough but I'd never followed it to the sea, nor had Nick. Here was our chance.

Leaving the openness of the basin there is little space for the river to wriggle. The opposing flanks of Beinn Dronaig and Carn na Sean-luibe that pinch its course are marked by burns and dotted with boulders whose spacing was such it seemed they must prevent the great skin of heather from being torn away. Beasts migrating downriver had chopped the peat into a narrow trail and we sometimes fell in with these ghosts but mostly our way mirrored the riverbank. It was a joy and unfolding wonder and in the early miles the Ling displayed every variety of flow, doglegs and twists that seemed bolted together with bedrock. It dropped to pulse through narrows and here the channel ruptured around a great stone capped in heather and divided three ways, each channel spouting water as if from a turbine-house. The boom of it hanging in the air. We climbed bluffs of dark grey rock at odd angles that offered no obvious way over, and tiring of this climbed to a small vantage and looked down onto the valley, the Ling broad and meandering across flats of grass and rush, this braiding to shoals and an isle of alluvium whose name is lost. Downstream the river sunk into a gorge with trees occupying crannies on each side and here it seemed like a serious mountain river in a region little visited.

Nick was especially careful at crabbing about the bluffs and moved warily, a hangover from yesterday. I found myself waiting a great deal. It was something I was used to and a feature of our journey together. Nick had come to it out of shape and had struggled. He was still struggling. Little of our walking was straightforward. I'd allowed for this when placing our caches but I'm not sure I realised fully the challenge confronting Nick when setting out from Dalmine on that raw afternoon. Nor how much he'd since risen, both mentally and physically, to face it. The wild trail I'd conceived through Scotland's west was of pathless moor and ancient wood, rivers to be crossed without the aid of bridges. Snow and high waters expected. I hadn't of course reckoned with sore feet but in truth no walker in winter can move with much haste anyway. Nor would they want to.

From day one our relative pace never married. For Nick a steady improvement in stamina was matched by a trimming of mobility due to his bruised soles. He never went noticeably quicker over the land and halts were the norm. I did nothing to jolly him along as I knew he was often at his limit. So instead I slowed and trod lightly and during enforced halts engaged more with my surroundings, visually and aurally. I could become drenched in a specific place. I'd always looked at the wild plants and small mammals and birds but in their lack I studied the rocks and lichen and colours therein. I grew to love the breaks and our slow working through the country and I saw how my impatience had perhaps stifled earlier experiences. Going slow was a new way of seeing and on a rock by the Ling I waited for Nick, hoping he'd spotted my last turn towards the river. It was chilly. I watched the trail of water funnel and run over a small drop and into a pool, waves reaching out and fading and recoiling in endless repetition.

I was looking for trout when a noise behind signalled Nick's approach. About a minute away. He followed my line almost to the step, bedrock to bog, slowed to make an awkward move and puckered his lips at its completion and came over to where I was sitting. I'd been there about ten minutes.

'Rough,' he said, slipping his sac from his shoulders. He looked about for somewhere to sit. The grass was wet and most of the rock had a pitted surface.

'Reckon I'll just sit here,' he said.

Nearby was one of those rusting iron stakes that had been set into the rock well over a hundred years ago. Of all the useless man-made features found in the hills these boundary fences stand pinnacle. Marching single-file over the highest crests they guard watersheds like rows of petrified stickmen, their original purpose to demarcate estate boundaries and to keep deer from wandering onto neighbouring turf. The wires have gone but the stakes are sadly enduring and often the only blemish you see in miles of wild country, a corroding oddity serving no purpose beyond a reminder of old fiefdoms. A message and a warning. Such a fence follows the Ling to Loch Long and extends east across the Ling Basin to Pait by Loch Monar, only the last miles of which are missing. Rightly pilfered and reassembled by the keeper for the restraint of his cattle.

One of the rusting posts had been hammered into a rock close to where we rested. Nick asked about them.

'Thomson mentions the fence. He said it took three hundred men to lay what was once the longest man-made boundary in Scotland. They used a thirty-foot barge to transport some hundreds of tons of iron, all coming in via Loch Monar.'

Nick studied the post up and down.

'How in heck's name did they get the barge to the loch?'

'I read it came from Attadale on the west coast.'

'Don't tell me they hauled it cross-country?'

'They did. With horses. They floated it where they could, on Loch Calavie and the Ged Lochs, but mostly it was dragged.'

'That's some effort.'

148

Nick shook his head slowly.

'Yeah, it is. Depending on the route they took that's twenty miles and a thousand feet of ascent and for something that must have weighed about three tons.'

'Just so the laird could shoot a few deer.'

'By all accounts he and his pals shot plenty. Local people and ghillies were paid to drive the deer into cul de sacs and there they were gunned down, often on the run. Massacred more like.'

Nick was rubbing his hands on some dead grass. There were some hinds on the hill opposite, all grazing, but they knew we were there.

'Hunting is inborn in humans, don't you think?' he said. 'Something reaching back to our origins.'

'Maybe, but we've come a long way from taking an animal solely for its meat.'

'You reckon we've gone backwards?'

'I would say so. The hunting we do now is driven by blood-lust and shows little respect for the creature targeted.'

'I don't know about that, I'm not a hunter. But I do know its popularity among the wealthy has resulted in the creation of large estates. The vast open areas we see today are a product of bloodsports. They say it's what folk love about the Highlands and why they visit. Ourselves included.'

'They would have you believe that, but given the choice I think most Scots and visitors would prefer more diversity, more trees and species. In terms of land-ownership the present picture is mixed. Venture capitalists with offshore addresses are now getting involved and their approach is to squeeze the land for all its worth. For its green energy potential and agricultural return. And of course the hunting goes on as before, only now they do it in the shadow of windfarms.'

'There's still wild places, still a few woods. As we've discovered.'

'True, and I'm heartened by this but have a look at the environment hunting has created. By managing these Highland estates for game, whether pheasant, grouse or deer, we've produced vast and nearly sterile tracts. Okay, some game birds need their woods but anything that might predate them is excluded. It's archaic.'

'Those who come to hunt bring millions to the Highland economy. It provides jobs where jobs are scarce. Ideals are fine if your livelihood is not at stake.'

The small herd were on the move, casually footing further up the hill.

'You're right about employment, of course,' I said, 'but don't knock ideals. We are creating something that from a purely selfish viewpoint won't benefit us humans in the long-term. It's caused by a cocktail of human-induced factors. Biodiversity allows species to exist within niches. Their populations rise and fall, but in general no one species will dominate. Not even a predator such as the wolf. By creating monocultures, whether for deer, sheep or grouse, we've also caused a massive vacuum. And all this exacerbated by climate change. Take the humble tick which can transmit Lyme's disease among other infections.'

'Ixodes Ricinus.'

'Is that the one? Well, as you know its numbers and range are increasing worldwide. Alarming for us humans. It's active for longer and is found higher and further north than ever before. Some scientists are claiming this minute creature will cause the first epidemic of global warming.'

'You're off on a tangent again. I've read all about ticks.' Nick laughed. 'Maybe I've read the same reports. But let me drag you back to hunting. I don't see a ban on it any of it soon. No government would see that as a priority.'

'Killing wild creatures doesn't do it for me. I used to fish when on holiday as a kid but we ate our catch or gave it away. Once I killed a sparrow with a catapult and it made me sick.'

'You eat venison.'

'I do, a little. But hunting is not culling, however these estates dress it up. It's part of our broader culture and few question it. Groups who want, say, a ban on driven grouse are portrayed as marginal and for now their opinions don't carry much weight. It's changing though. Years ago it was okay to kill wild-cats, otters and eagles. Only recently you could chase a fox to death with hounds. Do that now you'd be vilified, locked up. Rightly so.'

The deer were now a good distance away, save one. She was on a ridge-line, stock-still, staring at us.

'I guess it's about how we dispatch. Guns, yes, dogs, no. Some hypocrisy there.'

'Hypocrisy? Us humans? We're hardwired for that. Apart from say coarse fishing, hunting in this country is not mainstream but it defines how a small group of largely wealthy individuals view the land, to one narrow end, namely the quantity of game it produces. The rest of us in are complicit in our silence and we have the world we deserve.'

Nick stood up, threaded his arms into his shoulder straps and clipped his belt. He said plenty have it in for the hunting fraternity and he sympathised. But their activities are not always ruinous for the environment. Anglers for instance have been at the forefront in campaigning for cleaner rivers. And in France attempts to eradicate the emerging populations of wild boar are now being resisted by wild boar hunters, who rely on a healthy population for their sport. So it's not that simple. He didn't wait for an answer. He turned and headed along the riverbank.

The gorge was a place of waterfalls and rapids and we had no option but to contour high above it, then steeply down again to cross the sizable tributary of Allt a' Choire Dhuibh. Here an aged and dying birchwood among the broken fronds of last summer's bracken, all run through by sheep and deer. The Ling deeper now and flowing quietly and characterised by green pools in pale rock basins. A little further it was joined by the Uisage Dubh or Blackwater from the north, the flow of this water stronger as it had created a small ridge of shingle across the channel. At a roofless shieling we rested a good while and ate the last of our dry food and warmed some soup, the air cool enough for gloves. Only a few words shared as we sat on the soft grass and leant against the rough stone of the walls, sound of river across its gravel bed, a kind of seething, I closed my eyes and almost nodded off.

As we left behind the high country the bank was easier to follow and a path of sorts through ferns and myrtle, the river roaming wide where the land allowed, the shores gravelly and rapids fewer. A cairn had been assembled on a bluff, prominent like a beak or stone finger urging a safe direction. I climbed to it while waiting for Nick and watched an eagle on a rising arc then, as if something had caught its eye, it dived and circled overhead and shrieked. Food aplenty up in the basin. The great portal of Ben Killilan loomed at the gates of the valley and its outline grew dimmer as we neared but for a while we measured our pace against it.

By a large green barn, the first farm building we'd seen for days, we crossed a small bridge and a little further on in the fading light Nick bathed his feet. At that point we left the river and walked the track, primarily for Nick's feet but also because it had grown dark and tracing a meandering Ling with torches would be no fun and might even arouse suspicion. The glen is low-lying and benign and once much lived in but now deserted. Inbyes parcelled for livestock where crops once grew. Wild deer were much in evidence. At a muddy feeding station on the track a large number had lately assembled, their hoofmarks everywhere and a sour smell from an unseen carcass.

A night march it had become, for me an easy walk in the ruts and the earth slid past and my mind drifted until the moment I stopped and turned and watched for Nick's light, a mote in the darkness behind. Approaching so slowly on such simple ground. Wavering slightly. When I moved off again I tried to slow and check my stride, but it was actually hard to do and felt like dawdling so I pressed on and waited at stages. When Nick caught me up he trudged past saying little, only that we should keep going, and we marched like this for a good while, silent and as mismatched as two cogs pulling two levers on courses contrary yet calibrated to meet, and pass and meet.

At the last corner a light from somewhere in Glen Elchaig and something briny in the air as we lost height, now barely half a mile from the sea. In our fatigue and without thinking we turned inland onto a narrow estate road and there the grounds of the lodge and stalker's cottage. A security light pinged on. Dogs barking. We'd gone awry, but rather than retrace and re-alert the dogs, scaled a fence and crossed rough river flats and made ready to wade the River Elchaig which lolled like oil under our roving lights. A bad sign and no point testing its depth so we went seawards along its wild terrace, hands on ground, scrabbling and ducking groves of alder and wading an area of tall rushes and sinking deep into a peaty bed of a burn. A scramble up a bank and onto the narrow road bridge. Our food lay buried nearby but nothing was clear in the dark, especially as we'd concealed it in riparian undergrowth by the river and it was another hour before we found it.

I'd an idea to climb and camp on the high ground of Inverinate and tomorrow fashion a way among small lochs to Kintail, but Nick's feet had taken enough and we pitched up in a wood close to the road-end. I sorted through the cache. Nick said he was too tired to eat but when I combined tins for a meal he ate and he ate all three courses.

Nine

The night was starless and stony quiet, save when marked at intervals by a tawny owl. By first light the owl slept but now I heard the cries of marine birds, oystercatchers and gulls, a car or two as well on the small road below. So close to a sealoch the air felt balmy, this bucolic valley far removed from the cold hill country. I scanned the fringe of river and beyond to gorse and clutches of grey-branched willows and onto the slope above where birch ranged and amongst them the slash of a waterfall, its sound carrying up the valley. Only the snow-covered peaks of Sguman Coinntich and Ben Killilan on the far side reminded us it was still winter.

The sight of Nick applying plasters and popping painkillers did nothing but fuel a growing worry about the success of our venture. With a day's food only we headed up the road to the tiny community of Calas-luinie, a road-end collection of dwellings. Some vehicles abandoned alongside those new and some outbuildings crumbling. In small fenced plots lawns and shrubbery were a lush green and spoke of the clement air from the loch. An almost eerie quiet pervaded the hamlet, no one about, not even a dog and no one at the hamlet two miles up the glen where we crossed the river by a sturdy bridge and joined the main track. Empty fields here gnawed to the ground and even-aged stands of woodland run through with over-wintering cattle. A small group of them stood mute in trampled waste by a feeding station and watched us, their underbellies crusted in mud and one calf so covered he might have been rolling in it.

After a few easy miles we sat and made ready to ford the river. A lady jogger in a bright jacket came down the track and close behind were her two male companions, all looking fit and trim. Our conversing felt novel after so long alone and we swapped tales of the area. I didn't know it was half-term. They asked where we'd walked, the time it'd taken, how we coped with the snow.

The path promised to us by the map was a centuries' old escape hatch from Glen Elchaig and a shortcut to Kintail and head of Loch Duich, but it had no beginning and we had to rough-climb some way before finding its line. From here it carried us up the valley side in graded switchbacks, engaging the steepness with a ledge of laid stone and I didn't think ascending fifteen hundred feet could have been any easier. Nick caught me up. He said he'd enjoyed the climb immensely, though largely thanks to the path.

'A good path frees the mind,' he said between breaths. 'Plenty of time to think.'

'Ah. As if you need more thinking time.'

Nick laughed. 'Yeah, maybe.'

'But a path can also be a curb on ambition,' I said.

'How so?'

'I mean it channels its pilgrims into narrow corridors and you walk in others' shadows. Ghosts following ghosts.'

Nick stopped to suck water from a tube. He wiped his mouth.

'Well,' he said. 'I reckon they make walking a damn sight more pleasurable. You get time to appreciate your surroundings. Can't do that if you're always fighting the terrain.'

'Who said walking should be easy? We could have stayed at home.'

'Look, right now just putting one foot in front of the other is a challenge, path or no. In any case, paths are a part of the natural landscape. Been around for thousands of years, for as long as humans, longer if you include animal tracks. They follow lines of least resistance, like this one through the hills.'

'I get all that and obviously see how they improve access and how historically many of these routes were ancient rights of way for drovers and travellers, now enshrined in law.'

As I spoke I was captivated by a bar of light roving the hillside. A raven perched on a nearby rock seemed equally entranced but was probably just watching us and the valley. I paused, Nick also. We were both breathing heavily.

'They are also a tool of the landowner or authorities to herd visitors in a particular way,' I said. 'In National Parks where you mustn't leave the path, where you get corralled along a certain route.'

'Freedom to roam here in Scotland. No one is forcing you to use a path.'

'That's right. Like following the Ling yesterday. It was wild.'

'We didn't have any choice.'

'We did. We could have taken the path south over the watershed to the head of this glen. Would have saved half a day's walking.'

Nick stopped.

'Now you tell me.' He looked down at his boots. 'Sorry feet, I've been misled.'

'But the point is it's not about the easiest or quickest way. If your chosen way slows you and takes twice as long, all the better. It's the experience that counts. That section of river appealed because it's wild, well, for now at least. It was free-walking.'

'What?'

'Free-walking, a line guided by nothing more than an impulse or interest. Chase a whim. Sniff out a corrie, some waterfall up there, straggling woodland, on a crag'.

'Or follow a damn great river.'

The angle eased. Not far away a great squat boulder, tilted and leaning above the valley that was now fifteen hundred feet below. Nick was eying it.

'What would you give to see that thing go trundling down?'

At the pass a ragged and new land opened up. Retreating chains of mountains riding convolute east to west, acres of grey snow and dark terracing and the crown of each summit as far as Knoydart clear though entirely sunless, the land on a paling scale as if beset by a great shadow and all of it tilting back to winter. It moved me such that I said nothing. We sat both on a large stone and watched the light fade frame by frame.

In the dullness our path vanished beneath snowfields and when it reappeared we were led on a steep slant to aged and dark ranks of conifers and onto old forestry trails and into darkness. Accompanying us the boom of water as we went down on hairpins until the land levelled. A gutted building with graffiti and trash told of our nearness to the road. In another mile we were at the fringe of a pinewood and here I began a hands and knees hunt for our parcel. Nick searching close by. His blinking light coming through a matrix of tree limbs but I heard him more than saw him, a snapping and breaking like some creature hard-wired for clumsiness. I found a place with moss all scraped away and another with it layered and under this I found our food. The pinewood was too dense even to stand up in but across the track a slope of gangly birch offered better and here we set up our shelters. To soften where I would lie and to cheat the slope I wedged it up with moss and tied guys to surrounding trees. Nick pitched virtually where he'd stopped. Maybe his tiredness would allow him to sleep anywhere. I cooked a large and varied meal. At least we were eating well. A few feet from our shelters the ghost of a rill where we'd collected water, a trickling accompaniment to the boom of river in the strath below, though not enough to drown out Nick chanting a song from his player at some late hour and I couldn't help but listen, an odd tune crooned out like some canticle of old and not out of keeping with the muttering burn.

A dismal light in the tree cover and it was dark when it should have been light. I fumbled about with breakfast using my head-torch. Last night's rain still dripped from the canopy and the smallest touch of a branch triggered yet more. There was no undergrowth in this wood save moss and it was everywhere, covering the ground and climbing the trunks and wrapping them in green tunics like the faeries of old. Nick was up and moving about and I talked over our plans. I said we should rest tomorrow at the bothy as the day after involved climbing to the Five Sisters Ridge, an effort that certainly would try his feet. Okay, he said, a hand over his mouth to stifle a yawn, but let's stick to one day at a time. He said he felt a little fragile and didn't want to think about a big climb two days' from now. Let me just deal with this morning, he said.

The mountains were half-seen through the canopy though they ran true as we left the wood and took a narrow path, entering land newly planted with birch and rowan and in the ownership of the National Trust for Scotland. I'd not been on this ground for years but had heard something of the changes and read of their vision for restoring the old forests. The path contoured clockwise and on this arc and with the trees gone we started up the faded green slopes in a series of switchbacks. The architecture of Ben Fhada reared without a break. We tilted our gaze to ascertain how far down the overnight snow had come. From our stance I was struck at how high the hills seemed, on a scale greater than their known height. For a few seconds we watched three small figures in black way above us at the snowline and heading straight into the corrie. Climbers, I thought, for there were no walking routes there. A cold wind harried from the east and in that direction the sky was pale with cloud.

Without climbing to the summits the only way through to the east on this side of Fhada was by a defile known as Bealach an Sgairne. We were approaching the pass when I heard a click-ing sound. I turned to see a small rock spinning and bouncing and I watched it recoil and reach about head-height, recoil again and scuttle past maybe three yards away. A rock about the size of the palm of your hand.

At a burn just below the pass we stopped to drink and met one of the party we'd talked to yesterday by the river, and parleyed. He was on his own and said he was planning to climb A'Ghlas-bheinn, a little to the north. He pointed to a line that looped through the crags above our stance. I got out my camera and asked if he would take our photo and Nick asked what his employment was. An engineer. He spoke a little about it, saying his days were often filled with problems and his job to solve them. It could be demanding work, he said. He looked about. Hiking these hills could also be demanding but in a different way, maybe a more satisfying way. Here's a problem, said Nick. I've beamed you into the future when we are able by genetic engineering to alter the human brain. We can control at embryo stage someone's capacity for altruism. My question to you as a scientist is, would you be party to such an advance, one that might create a better society but in doing so reduce our freedom to choose, even undermine our free will. The man seemed taken aback but pondered this. He looked at Nick and again looked at the hills and turned and said it was not something he'd ever thought about, though adding that selfishness is not necessarily a bad thing. He said he believed some of the greatest inventors and pioneers of science were driven by a desire for recognition rather than a wish for a better world. And if so and given your scenario, where are the future pioneers? But to be honest I don't know. Maybe I come to the hills to hide from such questions. If you had my job you might too. He wished us well on our journey and he wished someday to undertake a similar journey, though that would be a selfish act, and with that he smiled and walked away.

The pass was so narrow I found it hard to believe herds of cattle were once driven here as records suggest. The defile itself was largely free of snow but descending the east side we heeled over great drifts and for a time lost the path. A broad elbow-shaped glen with a frozen loch and a solitary island lay spread before us, a sheltered upland haven and summer destination for the aforementioned herds. Gleann Gaorsaic ran to the north but we were headed east towards Affric and at the loch paused for a fine view over to Aonach Bhuidhe. The wind had dragged in low cloud and the hill crests on either side were disappearing. I have known this corridor to Affric as a waterlogged place and difficult to traverse, but the Trust had improved the old path and it lifted us dryshod over the worst of the bogs. I was some way ahead when I pulled up at an old fank and sat with my back in the lee of a wall and watched the hills and waited. The weather raw and cold now. The wind in the long grass and a slight whistle of it through gaps in the piled stone. I knew Nick was some way behind but couldn't see him. I should have kept a closer check on his progress. The waits were getting longer. When he finally appeared he was moving slowly and seemed to be favouring his right leg. This leg went forward and rolled out with each step, while his left come down uncertainly, as if the ground might give way. The accruing discomfort of it. He was breathing quite heavily and sometimes puckered his lips and he sighed deeply when he reached me.

'Sit down awhile,' I said.

'No, I'd like to get to the bothy. I can rest tomorrow.'

'Let's hope it rains then. Or snow. Get that out the way if it's coming.'

'No, not snow. That would finish me off.'

On the flank of the hill ahead what at first I thought was yet another group of deer were in fact saplings of a newly planted wood, the first such planting I'd seen in my decades of visiting. With Nick's feet in mind we stuck to the path crossing the Affric basin and reached the intersection of four glens, and here where the prows of great hills converge we swung right and southwest, an altogether wilder glen, and climbed a little until close to its watershed. On a good path the last miles were the smoothest yet slowest of the day. Light was fading when around the next corner the howff of Camban emerged from the dead ground.

The bothy has a certain ingrained profile in my mind born from how it is framed in a photograph. Sunrise on a September morning, the stone wall of the east gable hiding its length but the door ajar and a man standing there and he's looking to the North Shiel Ridge and Five Sisters, their hillsides brindled in the colours of autumn. That his only visit. I'd been many times and there'd been an upgrading since the early barren days, new bunks, tables, a bench, one room now partitioned. The ladder and sleeping loft were gone and I thought that a good thing as I'd once almost fallen through the hatch when descending in the night to chase a mouse from my food.

I warmed water and flicked through the bothy log book, damp and dog-eared though it wasn't old. The path outside is well-travelled and someone in an office had marked it on the maps and called it the Kintail Way to encourage yet more folk here. The scrawled entries spoke of the surge in visitors, but not in the months of winter. A man had reached here after the blizzard. He'd walked in from Morvich and had taken two days to cover the ten miles, the final two miles taking an entire day. I read back over the previous summer and it surprised me what some people had written. Like comments in social media. That we can be so mute in the face of the beauty. I don't know why I was surprised.

Nick went out to find some snow for his feet and we settled one in each room and as we were staying in a bothy I cooked for us both. Months of winter cold leaked from the thick stone walls and with no fire we ate our platefuls wrapped in many layers, hats and gloves included.

Nick was massaging his feet when he asked why I had chosen to route our journey here when we might have crossed the main road at Morvich, surely a quicker way to Knoydart. I said that was true but the shortest and easiest path wasn't the point of it. The journey was a grand meander, a thing of detours, a revisiting of old haunts though with some new corners to explore. I said in an age of leisure all journeys are contrived, but that doesn't make them any less real, or any less important. You ask about today's route? I wanted to cross the pass, a new place for me, and I wanted to return to these hills. They have mapped out my life and continue to do so and I want to be part of their story, a tale of woods and predators and glaciers and old regimes of fire and molten rock. And I once came here with Clive.

Night had long since fallen and beyond the walls a faint sound of wind and apart from that silence.

'There's an atmosphere here. Can't you feel it?' I said.

'Only thing I'm feeling just now is my feet.' And with little ceremony Nick sat and placed them in rusted pan of ice-water, grinding his teeth and calling softly to the rafters.

'I think it's the neighbouring ruins that do it. There's three or four of them dotted about here. One by the burn. When you're out collecting water there's a sense you're being watched. Nothing malign. Just a presence.'

'Thanks for that. You are acquainted with my imagination?'

'This high place like others was likely used for hundreds of years though probably abandoned for a time in the late 1780s when the summers failed. That happened across Europe. Frost fairs on the Thames and starvation here at the margins. These sour hills are a resting place for many, unmarked and unknown.'

'That's sad,' Nick said, and studied at his feet. 'Can you cheer me up please?'

I told him a story about coming here with a couple of friends, one of whom claimed the place disturbed him. Whisky had been consumed and I couldn't be sure if he was being serious. Anyhow I said that when the ruin was being renovated to a bothy in the 1960s the volunteers made a discovery. Two headless skeletons. Of course, the police were told and the police arranged for a pathologist to come and study the bones. The pathologist was puzzled and sent for an archaeologist. He said the remains were of great antiquity and that the unfortunate pair had likely been subject to a ritual that involved them being bound and gar-rotted. A sacrifice, he thought. My friend asked what became of the bones. I tapped the floor. Reburied, I said. Right here. He appeared truly shocked. But he nodded and said the story explained much and from then on refused to leave the bothy.

'Not even for a pee?'

'Not even for a pee.'

'What did he do?'

'Nothing, he just sat there and looked worried.'

'No, I mean . . . you know, he must have been in agony.'

'He used a peanut jar. And asked me to empty it.'

'Did you?'

'Of course I didn't. I told him I'd made the whole thing up. But he still wouldn't go out.'

'So no bodies?'

'No bodies.'

A crack from somewhere. The wooden partition answering to a change in temperature, an inside draught. Who knows. Later the only eyes on us were stars, so many and so beautiful after nights of cloud and I looked for constellations and rogue matter burning in brief flashes across the perfect blackness. Other worlds and other lives out there in the firmament and I found that easy to believe. It made me think about what the man at the pass had said. The epoch to come. I thought if humankind was to have a true flowering it will be predicated not on some ultimate conquest of nature but on a rediscovery of wonder.

The day brightened from the east and the snow peaks of the ridge lay stencilled over a blue sky. On the ground a covering of frost and in the burn doilies of ice extending out across slack pools. No wind and no noise save of water. When I went to rouse Nick I found him still tightly bound and unresponsive, headphones around his skull. I don't think he knew I was there.

So frigid was the air I retreated to my bunk and crawled into my bag and from its warmth orchestrated breakfast. Afterwards I lay for a time and watched the sun come through the solitary window and carry its frame elongate to the concrete floor, bright as magnesium. A scraping noise in the far room was Nick carrying a bundle of clothes and his tent to hang outside on a line he'd rigged. Then he took a chair and pressed it against the outside wall and sat in the sun, to read and think he said. I joined him with my own chair and we revelled in the novel warmth and sat in the sun's presence for a good while and hardly said a word, Nick with his face slightly raised and his eyes closed, as if in some trance and perhaps he was.

Old snow on the slope behind the bothy was blinding in the sun and poking through like strange aerials were hundreds of young trees, all planted in recent years by the Trust and part of their vision for a restoration of the primal woods.

When I first come here the only trees were solitaries among crags and in burn defiles, places grazing deer and sheep could not reach, the same across the Highlands. The arboreal survivors, though few, are crucial for a future forest as their seeds provide the saplings most adapted to this locale. Groups such as the National Trust for Scotland and the John Muir Trust aim to restore woodland by a combination of heavy deer culling and planting, a far cry from the policy of enclosing the remaining native woods with high deer fencing. I first saw such fencing in the late 1980s and now we see the result, a demarcated landscape, small plots of ungrazed amongst the desert of grazed. Woodland and moor. A sop to all interests though neither is natural.

Since the extermination of wolves the beautiful red deer have multiplied, their numbers fuelled by under-culling, winter feeding and milder winters. There may now be half a million deer roaming Scotland. There was not a day and barely an hour when we didn't come across them, solitary or in small herds, scratching at the undergrowth on the flats by a river, two luminous eyes caught in our torchbeams. So plentiful they barely registered. It's true you are going to encounter more in winter as they escape the heights, but they were everywhere. Over the years I've seen tens of thousands of them. I've only once seen a wild cat.

Cloud drifted in to claim the afternoon and a cold wind bothered the garments draped over the line, now trembling like pennants. I went inside for a jacket and when I returned Nick was unrolling his sleeping mat and placing it on the level space by the bothy. He collected his down bag and stepped into it standing and zipped it right up and lay down facing the sky as if in some protest against people coming up the path.

The cold sent me inside and I read the hours away and listened to the draw of the wind around the east gable. An aural backdrop I thought for those who once passed their lives here. It is recorded the last folk left soon after the First World War and I wondered if the sons had gone to fight and what they had felt on their return, if they'd returned, the long walk in army-issue boots from Cannich or Morvich. Rounding the last corner, seeing their old home. Ordnance and salvoes and cries of the dying replaced by wind and birdsong. The beauty and solace of growing up here against the blunt industry of war. Highlanders could be skilled marksmen and how is a deer or wild fowl seen through the sights different from an enemy soldier? Both in a kind of uniform. You would need to believe absolutely to do that, in your country, your cause, or maybe seeing your own kind so horribly mutilated was enough and the generals knew that, but in the reckoning such profound trauma can ripple through generations and damage kin a century later.

When I went out again a grey light was falling, the high snows pale and cloud scudding across the crestlines. The wind had risen. I'd not expected such a change and worried at what it might mean for our plan to scale the ridge and drop to Glen Shiel, the place of our last food dump and its unearthing essential if we were to continue. Nick was back in his room slouched in a chair listening to some lecture. He said the day had revived him in a way that cooped by Loch Glascarnoch hadn't. After days of cloud the early sun had felt like a benediction, and he said he would be ready for tomorrow's climb.

When I woke in the night the wind was still up and if I hoped it would ease by morning I was wrong. Loose grass and chaff in the air and high clouds driven westwards and brushing the podiums of the Five Sisters Ridge. I counted the seconds of their passing each with a single hand. The portents were bad. A lurid yellow light briefly over the high crests then all was grey and remained so. I'd woken Nick early but he was still asleep and snoring an hour later. I said the weather was going to break and we needed to make tracks, in fact we should have already. I'll give you a hand. No, he said with some irritation, I can manage. He did and by some miracle we were on the path heading west shortly after. I'd not even asked about his feet.

Windrows of dead grass had collected on the path and the gusts came from behind, a sudden seething that rose and sometimes we had to stop and brace ourselves to let them pass. The trodden way left the watershed and we kept a high line as the valley sunk and twisted to our left. It circled great spurs and in places was lost among snowdrifts, our steps the first over them. Glen Lichd continued to deepen, the hills on either side rearing up and growing in stature. I kept an eye on the truncated arm of Meall 'a Charra and traced its crest to the summit of Saileag and looked for ways we could safely approach.

When broadly in line we left the path and crossed the headwaters of the River Croe at the juncture of a smaller flow, before it ran into a chasm with dwarf trees bolted to its sides. Noise of falls echoing up as we climbed towards Am Fraoch-choire, the cold corrie, and crossed its burn above a bathing pool with greenish waters, a lovely place that in another season would have you pause but we hauled straight for the ridge, scrambling the steeper bits and picking among small rocky outcrops. Westwards a great land opened out. Beyond the chasm at the throat of Glen Lichd were the flats of the lower valley, the river idle in a series of meanders and braids and clamped by opposing flanks that soared without pause for three thousand feet, Beinn Fhada to the north, on our side Sgurr Fhuran. Trails of deer and sheep had shorn the land to its ribs, a scavenged place awaiting the return of trees. No shelter for any creature larger than a fist that doesn't live in a warren. The line of the path we'd so recently left now just a scratch and hardly seen.

At the snowline I waited for Nick and we proceeded each with an ice axe, the snow hardening as we climbed and the wind throwing us sideways. To counter its force we snuck a little below the crest, though on this more sheltered side the ground was steep and craggy and riddled with frozen meltwaters. With height the land unravelled, one mountain spine after another until pieced against the skyline the shelves of Torridonian sandstone and curved outline of the Fannichs and there the distant col where we stood ten days before. The visible world grew and it seemed to sway as if some upheaval in the crust itself but it was the wind shaking us, gusts hammering in from our rear quarter and with each we stooped closer to the ground lest we got slammed clean over.

Spindrift curled over north-facing cornices. The summit cairn was half buried and we were unable to stand upright and when Nick did he was almost lifted. For seconds we were frozen in our stance, heads bowed and turned away from the flying ice, all but impossible to look east along the ridge or to speak or make our escape. Nick sunk in on his axe and anchored himself, a leg each side of the cairn as if trying to tame it. He looked over and shouted something unintelligible. My plan from Suileag had been to follow the ridge west to Sgurr nan Spainteach, the Spainard's Peak, and from here I hoped to descend into Glen Shiel. There was no chance of that.

I cupped my mouth and shouted. We needed to get down, either the way we'd come, which was the safest, or we drop directly into Glen Shiel and into unknown terrain. No one I knew had ever done such a thing. Nick was shielding his eyes with a mittened hand. He tried to look at me. He said no to reversing the ridge, we had no food remember. So we went south, due south, onto a slope you would avoid save in an emergency. I reckoned this was an emergency.

I turned from the summit and wheeled away and after a few steps turned again to face the slope. I braced myself and begun slowly to kick steps. Below us was dead ground but a little to the east was some bare scree and we traversed across to it, hopeful it might offer a safer way, but it didn't. Our steps collapsed into the clinker and sent stones tumbling to be swallowed unseen some way below. I led Nick back to the snow and we faced the slope and kicked footholds. I didn't think of the huge slope below and didn't look either, just went on booting at the snow and swinging my axe.

Nick was just above my stance and using my steps to descend. I could see the length of the slope, all smooth and unbroken but the ground immediately below was still missing and I thought we might have reached the edge of some crags. I shouted up for Nick to work left and into the wind. Chunks of snow broke off with each step and were half lifted by the wind and tumbled into the void. Further left I saw the slope run out, a great blank field of snow that had frozen and thawed so its layers had mixed and I didn't think it would collapse. It was solid. If wind had lessened by this point I wasn't aware of it, deep in concentration, the kicking and placing of each foot, the striking of my axe.

When I looked back up again Nick was having no trouble following and was probably enjoying himself. He was so glued to the slope I couldn't see him falling. The snow softened, the angle easing a fraction. I turned to face the fall-line and walked down in great strides. Silent cars plied the road a thousand feet below, lights on as it was now growing dim. We were a long time coming down and towards the end were sinking two and three feet into drifts and still knocked about by the wind. On snow-free ground we traversed above the plantation, climbed a high fence and slipped through tall trees by way of firebreaks and where they'd been thinned by the Trust. In a mature stand of larch I surprised a stag. I thought all the deer of the hill would have found a home in the trees these last weeks.

For a time we walked an old soldiers' road that ran parallel with the main and stopped to eat the last of our supplies and count the last miles on the map. Dark cloud now shrouding the high ground, warmer with a light rain falling. Across the valley new fences protected the plantings of native species and even in the failing light the contrast between the browsed and unbrowsed land was astonishing. Nick's feet hurt but the wind was with us and the gradient all downhill and in a small pine-wood not far from the crashing sound of the River Shiel we set down our rucksacs and tried to remember where our trove of food was stashed. By a rootball of a fallen pine I recall, but there were many fallen trees and many rootballs so we went out on independent orbits, Nick's torch flashing among the trunks like strobes, the ground near swamp in places. We searched in the dark for a long time. Two trees had fallen together, their canopies still entwined and under their great root plates were signs of burrowing. We poked at the earth and uncovered our final and largest cache.

There was no ground suitable for two tents but we pitched anyway. Nick had given his feet such a hammering all he wanted to do was sleep so I cooked us a large meal and poured in tin after tin, soup, haggis, potatoes, green vegetables, coffee and tinned raspberries to finish. I cleaned my pans with moss and lay back and pushed my feet in the empty spaces of my sleeping bag, my head on a bundle of spare clothes and for a long time I did nothing save lie and listen. The slack drip of rain, the thrash of wind in the canopy, a more distant boom of waters in rising spate.

Ten

A singing in my head, some ballad of lost love that was pleasant for a time and I ran through the verses but even in my half-awake I knew the song would finish and the music end. Rising on its tail was the roar of the river, the noise caterwauling and distorted by a valley that rose three thousand feet on both sides. It appeared to have rained for most of the night and was still raining. I looked at the time and hardly believed it for the dark then remembered we were camped deep in a wood. The clouds also were low on the hills, what I could see of them. I mulled over our planned route. The immediate problem was the brute conveyance of six days' food over two passes. And whether Nick was actually going to make it. I judged if we could get to a bothy we could lay up a day or even two and buy time for Nick's feet.

Packing took a while because there was a lot to pack and when I hoisted my rucksac it felt heavier than at any time on the trip. A cold rain fell through the trees and everything in the wood dripped. Groups of deer had huddled here in the storm and their sour droppings pervaded the damp air. We wrapped in waterproofs from the start and so provisioned crossed the road to slant up the rough hillside, a graded path here marking the approach to the Forcan Ridge and Saddle. A party of teenagers cloned in bright red were ahead on the path, a laggard file of anoraks in the rain that vanished into the mist and we never saw them again. An elderly walker appeared all of a sudden. We'd not seen his approach as he ghosted into view on one of the bends. We stepped aside and he shuffled past, nodding, saying nothing.

The rain turned to wet snow that eddied like moths across the wild country of Coire Mhalagain to the south and where the Trust had established a young wood, the greens of native pines amongst the more muted browns. A covering of fresh snow could be seen through rain clouds and I was thankful we'd crossed the Kintail ridge when we had. The well-grooved path left the wood and ran at a fine grade below the peak of Meallan Odhar and towards the pass. At the snowline I turned my back to the weather and waited for Nick and watched the flakes pour over the valley and noted the rate at which the snow built up on the arm of my jacket, in a few minutes an extra weight to it. The heavy snow was erasing the footprints of the young party and at the bealach their prints were gone. A great remnant of the blizzard hung on this side of the gap and on it I scooped seats and watched blueish clouds smoking up the glen and speculated on what it might mean, ill or otherwise. The wind wasn't strong though and that at least was good. When Nick arrived he hardly said a word. He seated himself and chewed on some dried fruit. I asked about his feet and he just shrugged and said they were fine. A lie for sure.

With the snow thinning we went steeply into the lower corrie of the Saddle and at a more benign altitude stopped for soup by the burn. A great complex of cliff and headwall that make up the Saddle came and went, the Forcan Ridge notched against the pale sky like a great stairwell. We didn't linger over our soup. There were miles to cover and those miles in part rough and waterlogged and without a path. If a path did once exist here it linked those scraps of drier ground containing piles of lichened rocks among the coarse grass and ferns. Summer shielings from another age. Small bare trees grew sideways above the river where it had eaten down, the river gaining in volume and noise as it joined another that drained a ring of snow peaks at the southernmost reach of Loch Duich. Our way led west through a weakness in the ring but the river that we'd followed now barred our way. For a mile and more it churned past and offered not the slightest chance of a crossing. We were moving north, away from the pass. I showed Nick the map. He said we should have crossed higher up, when we could. Why didn't we? I said I didn't know, but look, there's a bridge. I thumbed the spot on the map. Nick leaned over to better see it. He looked downcast. That's miles away, he said.

Just a hundred yards or so ahead the river broadened to spread its energy over great spoils of dumped gravel. This was it. We untied boots and doglegged up the flow for many yards, stitching together shoals and braids and wading a final channel thigh-deep to a terrace and disused sheep fank, much broken. I sat on my rucksac and massaged my feet. Various floods had punctured the old fank into a waste of strewn rock, the trunk of a mountain ash stranded upstream of a wall. Before the coming of the sheep the path running alongside the river and swinging north to Glen Shiel was once taken by cattle on their journey from Skye to the market at Selkirk and beyond. The Trust have now planted a swathe of the valley with saplings grown from seeds of the last arboreal survivors. The place was slowly rewilding.

Following the drovers' route we bent into a series of switch-backs and climbed a thousand feet due west. I hardly paused to wait for Nick for he matched my pace. I was surprised at his workrate. Our steps were the only ones through the snow and at the highpoint by a frozen loch we halted. The rain had stopped a while back and clouds now thinned to reveal the peaks of the Five Sisters Ridge opposite, stripped of mist and bedecked in new snow. We sat and ate a little food and watched the climbing shadows, then in a late sun left the domain of Glen Shiel and picked down into a hanging valley. A softer prospect ahead with hills stunted by comparison, retreating to a coastal fringe, the first lands of Skye. A country of nibbled pastures and a strath floor still green and shaped into fields for wintering sheep. Conifers draped the higher reaches of Glen More and from one came the distant whine of a chainsaw. About three miles away on a sunny slope was a lone house, a dyke growing from the gable to mark out a little field, a single square claimed from the wild like the first homestead. There was no road to its door and from our approach not even a path.

On leaving the mountains the path was hard to follow and vanished altogether in deep heather above the river. We stopped at the ruin of a once substantial house, now barely more than a single wall, and walked on as the sun slid behind the hills and its stain leaving the snows on the Saddle. The sky deep-ened to indigo, Beinn Sgritheal lay stamped on banners of velvet. Stars had begun to appear as we reached the bothy and when I went to fill our pans the ground was already hoared with frost.

The wind rose in the night and I heard hailstones on the window, though by daybreak it was just raining and didn't feel as cold. Nick had billeted himself in the small middle room and I in the unfurnished one. We came together to eat in the room with the chairs and fireplace, as did all visitors it seemed. A vaguely repellent smell of rendered fat as if from a tanning yard though probably just weekends of folks' fry-ups. We had porridge and crisps for breakfast, the latter left by previous visitors. The salty flavour was extraordinary.

More foodstuffs in a cupboard and most dating from last summer according to scribbles in the log book. Cans of tomatoes, beans, dried rice and pasta, cooking oil that looked like cheese in a bottle. Even dogfood. For emergencies perhaps. Nick opened an old tin of coffee and sniffed it. He pulled a face and boiled water and made a cup and spat it out. There was a half-bottle of whisky that I thought was urine but wasn't and under the table the usual array of blackened pots and pans and a homemade trivet for toasting. I thought of the last time I'd eaten toast, or even bread.

At some point in the morning we donned waterproofs and took our empty sacs and made over the wet byre and ascended the conifer-clad hillside opposite. In a clearing we began picking through old brash lines. Cutting the seasoned logs with a blunt saw wasn't easy. The blade frequently jammed and we took it in turns to run it forcefully over the wet wood and had to finish some of the cuts by dropping a large stone over them. A great deal of effort but this scavenging for fuel seemed a natural thing in the circumstances. I crammed what I could into my rucksac and by the end its weight was near double what I'd shifted yesterday. Nick laboured close by. He said he wouldn't overload his sac like mine for his feet were supposed to be resting, but he did and like me rocked under the burden. When he fell over backwards he merely rearranged his load, tying some pieces on the outside for balance. It didn't take long. A month ago he would have been an hour at such a task.

Rain came on stronger as we worked up the slope and once inside spent much time grafting away with the useless saw halving the pieces for the woodburner. Nick made shavings with his knife and for a while we were both absorbed and focused on the matter in hand. If I stopped the stored cold of the bothy leaked from the walls and wrapped me in a private fridge so I didn't. The weather shortened the day and when it became too gloomy to see we lit candles in old beer cans someone had cut open and set on the wall to function as reflective holders. Not long after dark Nick set a match to the kindling. I was expecting our damp wood to be slow but the resin flared and warmth radiated and the world again seemed a bright place. I congratulated Nick on his fire-building. It's about preparation, he said. The core has to be true otherwise forget it. He spoke of favourite fires and especially those he'd had during a winter in the Canadian Rockies. Fires in the wilderness are both homely and a deterrent to bears, he said. I said I thought bears hibernate in the winter. They do, he said, but a mild spell can rouse them out and so roused they tend to be hungry and a hungry bear is a mean bear. You don't want to meet one, trust me. He said that unlike the Scottish Highlands the Canadian Rockies is true wilderness, untouched by any human agency and it prevails on its own terms. And he said these places are vast.

'You can't imagine how vast. Take the Northwest Frontier Province. It's twice as big as Scotland. Think about it.'

To demonstrate this Nick drew his arms wide and let them fall on the bench beside him.

'But I don't think that diminishes what we have here,' I said. 'You could be only a mile from a house or road and still be in a wild place, and in bad weather being a mile from safety is probably more dangerous than being deep in the Canadian outback, for there you have no illusions and most likely you're not there for a story but because you just want to be, maybe need to be. People pass their lives in such places and reckon nothing of it. Consider the first humans who came this way and scratched out a life here, the first human feet in these valleys. They weren't looking for a story or a testing ground, certainly not in the way we do today.'

'I've never doubted we still have wild places. And, as you say, the wind can make them equal to almost any place on earth, certainly in terms of harshness.'

'Why harsh? It's used all the time, a "harsh winter" folks say and pull a face. It sounds like a condemnation and maybe that's where we're going wrong. The Ancients would never have used the word "wild" or "wilderness" to describe the land. Probably didn't have it in their vocabulary. Everywhere was untamed and anyway untamed meant abundance. Wilderness was life. Their lives were rooted to the movement of animals, to the seasons, and they wouldn't have seen themselves as apart from nature. They were as connected to it as a tree is to the ground.'

'I don't know,' Nick said. 'Maybe, but we're second-guessing how these peoples lived by studying their few remaining descendents. They left no written records. Your notion they lived in harmony with the wild doesn't always match what we know. As you say there's evidence it was early hunters and not climate change that helped push the megafauna of the Pleistocene to extinction. The woolly rhino, great elk, the cave bear. All roamed Europe once. Humans probably chased the last mammoths to Wrangel Island in Siberia to die there diseased and undersized. There's plenty more examples.'

'I'm sure there is. But it didn't happen everywhere. The abundance Livingstone found say by Lake Ngami in 1849 was staggering. Sadly he opened it up to white hunters and millions of wild creatures were slain. Same with the American Plains buffalo. The world's ecology was in pretty reasonable health before we picked up a plough and starting herding animals. And for thousands of years even farming largely worked with nature and was often beneficial to wildlife though I guess the attitude of men seeking dominion over nature had been long fermenting, a biblical precept. Our language had by now framed nature as something different, to be controlled, and come the Enlightenment we began to develop the means to do just that.'

'Ah, the Enlightenment,' Nick said. 'Now that was a thing. The cold stare of the scientist.'

'It changed everything,' I said.

Nick reached for the water and filled his pan for more tea. The fire roared. I said although the ecological demise of the Highlands had been going on for centuries it was a slow demise. The industrial era by contrast heralded a new machinery of exploitation, whether hardy rapacious sheep or the excavation of a road and rail network, the land sold to title and opened up to speculators and its worth judged by the ledgers of moneymen. The windfarms and dams of today are just the latest instalments. It was a human tragedy as well, I said. Indigenous peoples with a deep feeling for their land were driven out or went on their own accord and joined refugees of the English Enclosures and factory slaves from the cities and great tranches of European poor destined for the imagined virgin lands and riches of America and Antipodes. The heartbreak of displacement and suppression of native peoples and the ruination of their lands repeating itself, a process continuing today and overtly sanctioned by voters in modern democracies and an ideology of material growth at all costs.

When I finished speaking the room was quiet. Nick was staring at the fire.

'Is that tea ready?' I said.

Nick shook his head. He leant over to the woodpile, selected a piece stripped of bark, and tossed it on the fire. He said it was a shame we agreed about so much because contrary positions often lead to new avenues, assuming of course those views are not entrenched. He said that as a research student you can't afford the luxury of unsubstantiated beliefs. For his research project he'd studied the spread of the plant disease Phytophthora on an area of heathland.

'I spoke to everyone using the area including dog-walkers, mountain-bikers, horse-riders. Everyone was aware of Phytophthora and how it was killing the bilberry. And they all seemed to know why it was spreading. The horse-riders blamed the dog-walkers, who, they said, allowed their dogs to run about untethered. The dog-walkers blamed the mountain-bikers. Their fat tyres churned up the soil, spraying it onto the vegetation, they said. The bikers, when I caught up with them, blamed everybody but themselves.'

'So who was right? What is causing it to spread?'

'Deer. Fallow deer to be precise, and here's why.' Nick closed his eyes as if to remember something he'd learnt by rote.

'Okay,' he said, 'after measuring the degree of interaction between the various potential disease vectors and infected heathland, and statistically analysing the data against the degree of Phytophthora infection, I found a statistically significant correlation between deer activity and the number of diseased plants.'

'Deer are to blame, then?'

'No, not entirely.'

'But . . . ?'

'But deer are the principal vectors of infection across the heathland. If you want to understand how the disease arrived in Britain then blame gardeners and plant importers. Blame globalisation.'

He said a species of Phytophthora caused the Irish famine, and another species caused five million oaks to die in Oregon. Neither were endemic to those countries. 'We know this from the meticulous gathering and interpreting of data.'

'Hard facts can turn people off,' I said. 'The reams of statistics about our impact on resources and natural habitats. Scientific jargon as well. You speak of correlations and vectors. That's useful among experts but if you want folk to reconnect with nature and rise up in its defence then I believe we need a new language. It's about appreciation, curiosity, joy. It's why children love nature. They see a flower. It's beautiful.'

Nick was quiet. He looked down at his bare feet and made small waving motions with his toes.

'I agree,' he said. 'So do others. There's a push to make academic literature more accessible by using plain English. But even when you put plain English in front of prejudiced individuals, perhaps those with money interests, then it doesn't matter what is true, only what you believe.'

In the small hours I heard rain on the windows and dripping in the chimney and I heard a mouse amongst empty tins on the floor beside me. Nick wandered in early with a mug of tea and said despite the wind he'd slept well. It felt milder than at any time since the north coast. With empty sacs still wet from yesterday we stepped outside and were shunted off by the wind down the brae towards the river. Just over the forestry bridge we found a quantity of fallen larch and wasted no time putting the saw to work, holding it by turns and hardly noticing the rain save when one of us stopped and watched it lance against the surrounding woods. Each log we cut double the width of the woodburner and all true so they packed into our sacs like bundles of posts and so heavy I had to heft Nick's sac onto his frame and he did likewise. Bent and climbing back up the brae, for some reason we drifted awry of our outward route so that the burn running past the bothy now needed to be crossed. Thirty-six hours ago I'd crossed in a standing jump, now I went upstream on rocks that broke the torrent, each step accompanied by a great swaying as my load tried to pull me over. I turned to wait and watch Nick, but then remembered so climbed the steep bank to the bothy. The hills had all but disappeared, even Torr Beag a quarter mile to the south just a wet outline and Beinn Sgritheal not seen in two days. My overtrousers leaked and once inside I began to shiver, so got into my bag to read.

When later I went to the main room I was greeted by a great fug of heat, the fire in the woodburner roaring and sizzling and Nick lying across the bench clasped in headphones and quite lost in music or the spoken word. He opened his eyes and gave his head a little shake and shuffled to make room. So warm we had to move the bench back and in a short while I exiled myself to sit barechested in the corner furthest from the fire.

The door of the woodburner was open. The fire spat and crackled. An ember fizzed to the floor. Nick was writing something, deep in thought. He looked up at the ceiling and seemed to study it as if a message was scrawled there then he looked over to the window that took the brunt of the rain and seawinds, a rapping sound of many hands. I thought we were pretty attuned to every crack and groan of this old house until there was a different sound. A distinct knock. Just one. We both looked sideways, as if expecting a rain-soaked face pressed against the windowpane but there was nothing.

Nick stood up. 'I'm going outside.'

'It's just something's come loose, a downpipe maybe.'

Nick was putting on his jacket.

'Or it might be a ploy to get us into the open. Either way shut the door behind you,' I said, half-smiling.

A clink of metal as the front door opened, a rush of wind. Torchlight flaring against the window. Nick came back, his jacket beaded and streaming.

'Don't know,' he said. He hung his coat over the line and sat forward on the bench, elbows resting on his knees.

I thought it strange that at home we bolt our doors yet out here feel safe sleeping in unlocked shelters and sharing such places with strangers, as if in the mountains we naturally drop our guard or perhaps realise we are too guarded in general. In centuries past hospitality had always been a given in the uplands, travellers offered space by the fire, a little food and a roof for their night's rest. In return the hosts might expect some tidings or a tale but the stranger was always welcome, well-heeled or ragged, for in the guise of a traveller might be Christ himself.

'We live in an era of private ownership when everywhere belongs to someone,' I said. 'And it all has a monetary value, at least in some calculable way. It's become a way of thinking about the world which is highly exclusive, a contagion that reduces land and resources to private or national control, and national is not the same as common. This bothy for instance is open to all. Its upkeep is paid for by volunteers, a registered charity in fact, but it has an owner and that owner can withdraw its use at anytime. Maybe renovate it as a holiday let or have it as a private bolthole. Nothing is for perpetuity. Scottish bothy culture is a throwback to the idea of common ownership or shared space, but it's entirely reliant on the whim of landowners. It's a system at the cusp.'

'I think it will change,' Nick said. 'The numbers using both-ies are growing. Time was when only those in the know could tell you where they were. Now you just have to switch on your computer.'

'A good thing in general, more people enjoying the hills. We can't keep them for ourselves. But bothies are a fragile resource. Imagine arriving here on some wild night and finding it full to the rafters, as I did once. Hardly floor space to lay your head.'

'I've seen it myself. So maybe we need wardens or some sort of booking system they have in the Alps.'

'And money will change hands. A type of privatisation then? That would be a shame.'

'What's the answer?'

'More bothies. The Highlands is dotted with ruins from the sheiling days. Many could be rebuilt and each in its own ver-nacular. These remote dwellings were put up for local folk and their laughter filled them, so why not again?'

'A great thought,' Nick said.

I hoped to reach the sea today though that largely depended on Nick's feet. He said he was down to his last painkillers but also said he would reach Kinloch Hourn no matter what, pain or no. I packed my rucksac and waited out a hail shower then went outside to bide time. After all the rain the land had a fresh look and for a brief minute an unexpected sun wrung out the last colours of winter, the crown of the Saddle winking in fresh snow. Through a gap in the hills Beinn Sgritheall rose clear and seemed like a tent whose ridgeline had sunk, its corrie with the shadow of its south summit projected onto it.

The track below Torr Beag was so puddled we walked the rough moor instead, climbing to the watershed and a flooded Loch Iain Mhic Aonghais which sat astride it and further on to cross a lively burn. A strange brown rock midstream was in fact a dead deer floated down in the spates. At the head of Gleann Beag we split from the main track and began climbing again, leaving the last of the planted conifers and for a few miles drew alongside a row of pylons all cloned and reassembled and set at intervals up the glen. A bleak and empty place, dark clouds closing over the hills and tipping out their hail and sleet as we walked head-down to the pass. Once a cattle-droving route and now a Right of Way, though a little-used one going by the lack of path. Broad and grassy, it rose in gentle stages and I could see why for centuries it was a favoured route for cattlemen. I wondered at the numbers of beasts that came this way and tried to imagine them, a milling herd of black and horned cattle, small in stature by present standards but muscular and powerful of leg and with glossy coats born of rich Highland grasses. The drovers at the rear and outer in chequered plaid and blue bonnet and armed with pistol and sword against the wild men of Knoydart through whose lands they would pass and whose foremost business was larceny. Hooves chopping the soft turf, their manure greening the halts. They'd swum buttoned nose to tail across Kyle Rhea from Skye and were herded up Gleann Beag past the ancient brochs, themselves in the shadow of earliest nomads and settlers to these parts. The drovers a kind of nomads themselves, the last people in Britain to journey on foot for their living and the last of them little more than a hundred years ago.

With rain coming on I turned my back and watched Nick's slow approach, hunched over in the mist like some early form of hominid. The broken gable of a sheiling lent us shelter and we brewed tea and saw out the shower. A final steepness before the pass, then in front of us a new land. Spurs and tumbled ridge rising over ridge, the land generally rock-strewn and shorn of soil and deeply scarred. A fresher green clung to the lower glens and towards the coastal margins old woods still grew like coverings of fur and despite the pylons it presented a wild and lovely scene. Here were the approaches to Knoydart and as I studied the view something came back, a fleeting thing but tangible for that. As I looked about for a nook on which to sit the sun broke through and the grey puddle at my feet reformed into something molten. Its surface creased in the breeze, then went smooth again. In a corridor down-country there were innumerable pools, sallow or grey or points of light, like mirrors over which the sky passed. A nameless thing of place, but I've never been here before. Nick crested the rise and the moment was gone.

If you left the pass and brushed the head of Glen Arnisdale you could by small defiles and trending southeast reach Kinloch Hourn in seven or eight miles. The pylons mark the old route today but it was never my wish to follow it and instead we dropped to the west and into Coire Chorsalain, entering a small hanging valley. A roughly-made track now reaches this high place and for no real purpose. The valley was marked by an abrupt steepening and over this ran a waterfall. Rocking slightly in the wind, I stood at its lip and stared into a cavity, the waters freefalling and thunderous until a sudden updraught made them twist and reverse back into the corrie. My face streamed.

Nick was slumped on his sac chewing some raisins. He looked over.

'That's some drop.'

'You can't see it from where you're sat,' I said.

'Don't need to. I can feel it.'

'Yeah, it's almost like a fissure. I wonder if it's well-known, if many people come here.'

'Not on any tourist route, is it? So I doubt it.'

'We're not far from the road, but the walk to here is a hefty one. But then I wonder if the effort to reach this place changes the way you see it. I mean compared to coming here in a vehicle, which you could probably do in a 4x4.'

'I don't see why. The view's just the same. It's a strange logic that says you cannot appreciate a landscape unless you put in a shift to reach it.'

'I didn't mean that, only I think you see it differently.'

'Drop me here by chopper next time and I'll see if differently for sure. For one thing I won't be knackered.'

By now Nick was lying back with one hand behind his head. With the other he continued to feed himself raisins.

'Are you going to take a look?' I said.

'Nah, let's get going.'

The track's hairpins had us looking down on the river amongst stands of birch, all dead or dying and bisected with animal trails.

At its steepest we seemed to hang above the grazed flats of Glen Arnisdale, the river coiling and slow between its gravel beds. On the banks and pasture were shapes of ghost rivers, fading oxbows and sunken lanes and waterless for a thousand years but remembered by the land and printed in bas-relief like a language for birds. In waning light we crossed the flats and stopped to watch the lights of a vehicle on the far side of the river, a sleety rain now falling. We hid from the wetness in a kind of barn. I looked up at the solid roof and said, shivering, why not spend the night here. Nick agreed, conceding his feet were such he wasn't able to go on in any case.

With dinner cooked and eaten we opened the map on the floor and examined our route along the north side of Loch Hourn, an eastward toiling of the coast that marked a good many miles before any road was reached. I knew of no one who'd been there. Nor did Nick. I'd often studied this section of map, the jagging shoreline and bunched contours, skerries and woods, all of it deeply appealing. But I'd had never set eyes on the place. Maybe I was saving it. Paths nibbled at both ends but did not meet, though I reckoned they once did. Ruins were marked here and there and at two sites buildings of a sort, boltholes I guessed, sanctuaries at the Atlantic's edge. It seemed like a last wild place and it was the only way I wanted to reach Knoydart.

Someone had spent the night here before, as on the dusty concrete floor were a couple of half-burnt candles, squat like the type you see in churches. To save our torch batteries we lit them and beneath a great vault of cold rolled out our mats and sleeping bags, a candle each and the flames unsteady in small draughts and painting Nick in garish forms. He lay mummied up on his back, his eyes closed, lost in some lecture though it was hard to believe he could listen over the strafings of hail on the metal roof. When it quieted Nick asked me about Clive. How had I known he'd gone to Knoydart? I didn't know, I said. Nobody did.

'The police had got onto me because I was often out with him,' I said. 'I knew Clive would happily drive a big distance for a walk. He'd go to Sandwood Bay and back in a day. Maybe he got that from being a journalist, you know, chasing the story and putting in the road miles.'

'So what happened?'

'Well, we needed to find his car for starters. His disappearance was reported in the press and his many friends began to post messages and urged anyone on the roads to keep an eye out for his silver Volkswagen. By Tuesday morning pretty much everyone in the Highlands had heard or read the story. I went to work but spent the day taking calls. Friends and family, and the police as well. It was surreal.'.

'How were you feeling?'

'Frustrated, anxious. I think people thought that I had some insight into Clive's actions but I honestly didn't know. I was ready to drop everything and mount a search but couldn't do a thing until we found his car. The lack of news was maddening. I remember thinking, how difficult can it be to locate his car? But you trust the police. There was a plane out looking for him. One story was that he'd come off the road and rolled into a ravine somewhere, hidden from view.'

'I remember getting your text. I still have it.'

'I tried to keep everyone in the loop. I was getting calls and messages from folk, friends and colleagues of Clive from way back, some who I'd never met but who were deeply fond of Clive. You could read between the lines. Their anguish was real.'

'What were you thinking in terms of where Clive had gone? We know he used to just take off.'

'I'd sent the police a load of grid-references, mostly of places we'd been together. A lot of them in the northwest. There were so many. But to be honest I was a little short of ideas. Clive was spontaneous, he did his own thing. He didn't always like to return to a place, especially one he'd been to recently.'

Nick knew the story as I'd talked of it before, but maybe not in such joined-up detail, the cold chronology as it unfurled.

There was a lull in our talk. Nick went back to his head-phones. I thought of the weeks before Clive going missing. I remembered he'd been snowed under at work. The routine of working alone in a small office as a sub-editor and journalist on a small weekly newspaper, sifting and shaping the mountain of copy in a rush for the printer's deadline, then to begin the process again, the endless cycle of news-gathering. His one proven way to relax was to take to the hills or maybe a beach and I knew he wanted to go somewhere that weekend but, given the conditions, didn't think he would. I didn't think anyone would.

Tuesday morning was probably too late but I filled a flask anyway and with Anne headed north over Kessoch Bridge, west at Garve junction, my stomach churning and a strange sadness that the bright spring weather seemed only to deepen. If he'd gone out on such a day he'd have come back, I thought.

Loch Achanalt on the road to Achnasheen was frozen, the higher hills under cloaks of snow. We began by checking laybys, parking bays, sidetracks, not all of them visible from the road. Our tyres crunching tree foliage and small branches brought down over the weekend. From Kinlochewe and on towards Torridon. After months of winter Beinn Eighe and Liathach were without compare but we didn't stop, not until winding a way to Lower Diabeg where the road ends and in a south-leaning nook the first daffodils were flowering. Over the waters in crisp outline the volcanic spine of Skye and knuckles of hills beyond, the Clisham on the Isle of Harris. Hardly a puff of wind and warm in the sun, the arrangement of hills and sea in such clarity would have seared it as a memory for other reasons. You could wait months for such a day. It was hard to conceive of Sunday's storm that fought the incoming tide in a chaos of breakers.

If I'd left home that morning with a flicker of hope it had entirely gone by evening. His car had still not been found. I was sure we were not looking for Clive anymore.

A report that evening came through that Clive had been photographed by close-circuit television heading south towards the A9. I thought that strange. He commuted every day to Aviemore, so why on his precious weekend would he head in that direction? But he knew the area well and we'd approached the hills from many of the roadheads, so against my gut feeling I drove alone to Whitewell Farm in the Cairngorms and walked a little way up the track. A grey and bitter day. I stopped at the gate that marked entry to a pinewood. Branches torn off in the storm and pine needles everywhere. A memory here of a winter's evening after a long day on the hills when Clive had lost a lens from his glasses and with torches we'd searched the long grass by the fence-posts. Probably still there. I drove the long narrow road through Glen Feshie to Achlean and halted at the small carpark. Only a few other vehicles on this cold weekday and by one a group of ski tourers fussing over their gear. West-aligned corries bulged with snow beyond their normal proportions and it all betrayed a storm from the east. On the ground was strangely compacted snow, difficult to walk on, and I realised it had been blown in from the higher slopes over the weekend and piled here. I thought of the billowing clouds of drift and freezing winds and tried to imagine Clive coming here and setting out but couldn't. At Feshie Bridge I swung left and followed the west side of the river, the road deteriorating and becoming an estate track. Tracks led off into the forest and I thought it strange that in years of coming here I'd not really noticed them before. But why would you drive up one? I checked old haunts by Kingussie and Newtonmore. Loch Garton was a sheet of ice. A birdwatcher there with huge binoculars. For lunch I parked up and bought his paper, the *Badenoch and Strathspey Herald*, and read a long piece on the search and included were comments from a number of his friends that sounded like tributes. Clive had now been missing for four days.

On a whim heading home I took the narrow road by the Dulnain, the river low and clear but it carried only a grey sky and light falling snow. Tiny flakes melting instantly. I turned for home. The evening news confirmed his car had still not been found and that a spotter plane had all day been roaming the skies above the Highlands.

The empty experience of searching the Cairngorm fringes further convinced me that Clive had gone west, so on Friday we went west again, this time heading for Gairloch and the Loch Maree area. The lovely brightness had returned and my mood must have shifted to some kind of preliminary acceptance because I was moved by the sheer beauty of the Fannichs in morning light and tiered architecture of An Teallach. We drove near-empty roads with no great sense of urgency and stopped often, sometimes just to look at the view. At the few shops and hotels we left 'missing' posters. We called in at Gairloch police station. They said they'd checked the road-end at Melvaig and Redpoint but we went anyway. Further down the coast we parked up at sandy beach and threw sticks for Hollie and set up a picnic in the shelter of a dune. My phone rang. Clive's editor in Aviemore. He said Clive's car had been found. At Kinloch Hourn on the edge of the Knoydart peninsula, possibly the remotest hamlet in mainland Britain. Two mountain rescue teams had been alerted and were on their way. Knoydart was one of the few places in the Highlands I'd not been to with Clive.

Eleven

In early morning hail rattled the tin roof and woke us and later we breakfasted through more showers and waited out another before moving, both pleased to be away from the cold and damp of the barn. The ground half-white with hail and it was like the early days in the north, now recalled almost with nostalgia. A fuzz of winter woodland extended inland up Glen Arnisdale, a natural unkempt look to it, the land rising by spurs and shoulders to a defile some miles away. The call of something feral and disorderly but we crossed the river and turned towards Corran. An old sycamore with great knotted roots growing solitary amidst the grazings. I wondered about its age, the changes it had seen. The hail eased to a fine drizzle and through the murk and across the water the hills of Knoydart reared their full height, preened in overnight snow. When that tree was young the house by the river was lived in but now its tin roof was down and rooms full of rubble. A piece of farm machinery aging prematurely in the salt air, a rotting trailer as well.

The hamlet of Coran is at the end of the road and a long road at that and deserted this quiet winter's day. Not even a parked car. The houses though appeared to be occupied and the first we'd passed since those by the Ling more than a week before. A caravan To Let, then the last dwelling and finally a boathouse. We crossed saltings and a tidewrack of squishy kelp that ponged mightily and we left the beach for a snaking and ragged path through coastal woods. What trees still grew on this south-facing coast clung doggedly to the land. Oaks a foot or two high and clipped by salt and seawinds, trees in every stance, their frames arching over the earth and still holding last season's leaves, trunks smothered in moss and lichen and branches in polypody ferns. Birch and bone-coloured ash and low-growing willows and among them the glossy leaves of ilex, some very ancient, their grey skins always bare as if from a kind of allelopathy. Much about the path suggested it was once an important way. Laid over shoreline rocks, sea-hammered and blueish, the gaps carefully fitted with regular slabs and sometimes tiered up to keep the walkway more or less level and above the reach of tides. In one place we squeezed through a small chasm with a slight echo and in another picked along a kind of ledge. Abandoned crofts might explain the path, turf-topped dykes marking small plots now gone to grasses, dried stems pitching in the breeze.

The earlier clearance south was but fleeting and Ladhar Bheinn and her acolytes across the lochs remained in cloud and eased by unseen and during showers even the loch disappeared. By early afternoon there was a growing brightness and no more showers, which was just as well as the path had gone and we fought through boulderfields and scrub. Pieces of cliff had slid down or peeled off in large flakes and lay surprisingly regular, as if from a ruined temple, we to clamber over them. We sat on the beach for a brew and watched the flood tide run past skerries and swirl in gouts of foam. The speed of it was impressive. It would be inundating the flats at Barrisdale Bay opposite and piling up the narrows to Kinloch Hourn. The waters were empty of craft. I thought of the herring fleet anchored here more than a hundred years ago, so many boats crammed into the narrows they said you could step from deck to deck and cross the loch. They chased herring shoals that were reputedly five or six miles in length and three or four wide, so large they would have blocked sunlight reaching the seabed, a seabed six feet deep in herring eggs. The herring themselves pursued by enormous cod, tuna, blue and mako sharks, fin and sperm whales. These monsters hunted in coastal lochs and inland seas of the British Isles that were likely crystal clear due to vast numbers of oysters and mussels and because the land had yet to be deep ploughed and deforested. A time of almost unimaginable abundance. Almost all gone. I remember Scottish beaches alive with crabs and clams, rockpools packed with colourful life as depicted in a child's picture-book. I remember it on a beach not far from here.

At our feet the mulch left from previous tides was like the mucus trail of great slugs, or maybe a bleeding from the earth itself, and it showed all manner of human waste, mostly plastics, containers and bottles of every type. A laundry basket, nylon rope, buoys, bags. The detritus of consumption. I knew there was more that we couldn't see, the microbeads and nurdles and the tiniest fibres. Heavy metals poisoning fish and maligning food chains. A shock after the clear burns and wild camps where you might go a week without spotting so much a sweet wrapper, though I now read windborne polythene scraps are to be found even there. I looked at it and looked across the grey loch. Such waste had been reported everywhere, trash on oceans thousands of miles from here, trash in the deepest trenches.

The small headland of Caolasmor confines the loch to just a couple of hundred yards or so in width. A little beyond this and nestling in its lee were a couple of private cottages, a rope swing on the tree, jerry-built stone bench and a firepit. The aforementioned boltholes seen on the map. An escape from the world, but there is no escape, not from the rising waters nor from their toxic cargo.

The last miles had been slow and light was fading. It had also begun to rain. On shorn grassland at the tip of the cape we set up camp, the cold wetness thwarting our plans for a fire. After a shared meal I read a little and listened to the acoustic of rain on the fly, the quiet whistle of breeze through the guys. Sounds of comfort and of other camps and maybe one where the tent was of canvas, the guys of rope and the pegs carved from great plugs of wood that earlier I'd pounded with a mallet. In a meadow by a high embankment on which goods trains rattled all night.

There were other sounds. Waders and gulls and a type of crow and a waterfall on the coast opposite and the quiet lapping of waves over the shingle beach, the tide having reached its turning-hour.

The sky must have cleared because the rain stopped and temperature fell. Stars appeared in the reaches above the mountains. I thought of the coastline across the loch which held a worn and lovely path and where nearly two years before we'd searched for Clive. It was at about this point that we turned around.

With the finding of Clive's car I didn't think it long before we found Clive himself. The great Highland-wide cordon had closed to a point on the map, where the sea met the mountains. I'd joined a small group of Clive's friends and drove in convoy the twenty narrow and winding miles from Invergarry. This was no reunion and a curious atmosphere in the vehicle, people I knew and liked yet not seen in years and one I'd never met. The talk all about where Clive might have gone and why on such a day of storm. And matter-of-fact logistics, where to search first, timing of our return. I thought everyone knew what we'd be looking for, yet when I studied their faces I couldn't be sure.

The road reached the dam wall at Loch Quoich and from the sides of the reservoir reared the barren hills of Spidean Mialach, Gleouriach and Gairich, a land stark and shorn of green after the long winter. I'd never seen the loch waters so reduced by drought and frost, in their place a great dirty ring of bare rock, gravel and mud. I didn't think that would have drawn Clive but he'd seen it and driven past, the last miles he would ever drive. At Kinloch Hourn is just a single house, a pier and boathouse and beyond this a rocky path west, half a dozen miles to the keeper's cottage and bothy at Barrisdale and half a dozen more to the high passes and peninsula of Knoydart. The coastal path is the walker's favourite. Alternatively you might cross the river to the lodge where paths radiate, an old Right of Way to Glenelg, another north to the wild country of Kintail. Or you might not take a path at all.

Clive's silver hatchback was already gone. As we pulled up a small group from Kintail Mountain Rescue were milling about their landrover. They were back after an initial search the previous evening and we discussed Clive's possible routes, his state of mind, the weather on the day. They'd gleaned from a resident the wind had been so strong over the weekend no boat could be launched and the keeper had been forced to walk the coast path to Barrisdale. He doesn't remember seeing a lone walker. As the team had already combed the ground to the north and east we all struck out on the coastal path, the red-jacketed rescuers and their collie to the fore. The first stretch corrals you along a natural ledge that stares directly onto the tide wrack at the loch's head. Beyond this we left the path and dropped seawards and began to trace the actual shoreline.

I counted the times I'd been here before and with whom. A bright place in my memory but now the land presented itself more as a riddle, of how it might hide somebody. In ones and twos we fanned out though always within earshot. Each wayside vantage was reached and studied, each bluff climbed and descended, their footings scoured for any sign, coarse grasses and dried mud in the hollows. A strange business, this searching for your friend, he so fresh a memory, his laugh and easy manner. Two of us went pawing up a vegetated cleft and at the top looked back down. Would that have been fatal? Rocks to hit on the way. I tried to gauge where a falling person might come to rest. That and other scenarios. We poked among ruins and combed the outbuildings at the empty house of Skiary. Warm in the spring sunshine and in spite of the chill and lingering frost I sweated. A near flawless sky and in any other circumstances a perfectly lovely day to be out.

All day I feared what we might find and I wondered who the finder might be, which of us, or maybe one of the Kintail group with their greater expertise. So much rough terrain and so easy to miss a man lying silent and still. The equinoctial sun cast hard shadows and glinted on high frozen burn-lines. I shielded my eyes to study them. Clive loved waterfalls, especially frozen ones, and there was one just above us. The climb to reach it was icy and steep, dangerous on such a day. There was nothing there and nothing at the base of some very steep and broken slopes, so we moved slowly on towards Barrisdale. Beyond the old walls of Runival and where the loch looks over to Caolasmor we stopped for a late lunch and mulled over options. From here the path turned and began to climb inland. In another mile you would see Barrisdale. The Kintail team were not far away and came over to join us. Their faces serious and sympathetic. One had a theory that Clive had fallen from the ledge onto shore rocks, his balance taken by a gust and he carried away on the ebb tide. Plausible but I didn't believe it. There was a general discussion about the importance of leaving details with someone when planning a walk in the hills. Even an impulsive one. I agreed, but said it was not always possible. I said I once spent two weeks in a range of hills near here. I had no phone and no contact with the outside world. I was due to appear at a certain place on a certain date but had I not then I might have been anywhere. If a single square mile can take a day to search, what of five hundred square miles? One of the rescuers asked if I'd left a route-plan. I had, but my route changed day to day and varied according to conditions and in the end bore little resemblance to what had been written. The rescuer nodded. He said over the years people go missing in the hills and are never seen again despite extensive searches. I said I'd heard of such stories. It's tragic for their loved ones but there's also a kind of comfort, for who would not want this arena for a grave and for one who so loved these places. But they were just words.

With Barrisdale around the next headland and the tide ebbing we turned around. We thought about spreading out again, there was still time, but some in our party needed to get back. We'd come five miles by the path. Nobody seriously thought Clive had got this far. At the carpark we met the Kintail group again. They'd climbed to the base of a high frozen waterfall and scoured its margins. One of the team and the search collie climbed the ground beside the icefall for a last look when the dog lost her footing and tumbled twenty feet and now limped badly. At the head of the loch were a couple of RAF mountain rescue vehicles and a trailer with a large inflatable and double outboards. Driving back we pulled in to allow a police car to pass. More traffic on the lonely road than all winter.

We all gathered at a friend's house in Invergarry and enjoyed a lovely meal provided by our hosts and talked over the day and maybe what we would do next. I was disappointed we hadn't found him but also relieved, for who wants to see their friend left to the weathers and in such a state. When I left for home it was night and the miles along Ness-side were the worst of the week, a road so familiar when the miles were shared but solitary and dark and haunted over by such an incalculable absence and a sense of the world turning and the past forever coloured. We were all too late.

Twelve

In the still air a deep chugging grew in volume, a small launch heading seawards and I thought its movement at first light was all about the tides. The timbre of it opened a door and time seemed to collapse. A childhood spent on boats and the metronome of the engine in early morning as I lay half asleep in the cabin. Those summer dawns on the west coast when we left on the flood. The engine suddenly stopping and in the new quiet the boat leaning and we running under sail, caress of wind and click of waves against the hull. Not one particular morning but many and I lay there and thought of my parents because that was forty years ago and they'd been sailing ever since and were sailing still.

A rain shower passed, then more sunshine. Birds busy with their calling, gulls and curlews out on the muddy shingle and I wondered do they abide here, a witness of the event, and what had they thought of a creature not on a food quest? The folly of humankind. I noticed for the first time a number of insects had invaded my tent, tiny spiders, the odd fly. I studied some ground beetle on the ground sheet, shiny black abdomen shifting side to side, head down, antennae twitching, mandibles thrust forward perhaps in a hunt for the spiders. The articulation of its six legs was extraordinary. I helped it outside and watched it vanish among the broken fronds of bracken and wished it well. I looked over to the cleft above the bay where birch trees grew and I thought of those trees as part of a green corridor stretching unbroken to the north coast, marking the line we'd walked and other lines, broad enough for all creatures to pass unseen and elevated at each road crossing. A small concession for beings, stateless and without allegiance, yet whose right for space is as intrinsic as ours.

For a short minute the sun warmed the inside and it felt like the first breath of spring. Then it was cold again, a perishing wind from the snows. Nick's vestibule open and flapping. I called over but he didn't answer. I knew he had suffered by his feet and not only that. The physical discomforts, the trials by nature, the tiredness and sheer effort and occasional danger. But they are largely forgotten and in the last only a small part of the tale and nothing to what he'd been through.

The wind in small pulses. Across the loch and towards its head were stands of pale and thin birch and the bottle-green of Caledonian pine. I could see the walls of Ruinval in its faded meadow and a lone alabaster pine, forked where its trunk gave out and long dead. A silent waterfall above.

I got up and went to see Nick who was muffled up in his sleeping bag. I said I didn't think it was that cold.

'It isn't,' he said, 'but I left the door open to feel the wind on my face.'

'You mean your nose. That's pretty much all that's showing.'

Nick asked about the day's plans and commented on the beauty of the coastline, something he'd not expected from his study of the map. I said in some ways maps are the poorest of all representations. Old maps carried the mapmaker's character but modern versions are merely abstractions, products of the computer. They are a tool only. Useful in a practical sense but I can't get romantic about them. We say they're detailed but they're not. At a scale where a thumb covers a mile they can't be. Those who see them as art or something special are misled. Their intention is to dispel mystery, not garner it. In fact I believe they act as a barrier between the user and the landscape. Nick said all that might be true, but he still loved maps. He said there could be beauty in abstraction, in the juxtaposition of symbols, in the legend. Pictographs for a people whose usual preference is for words. But anyhow, he said, what is the plan? There is no plan, I said, save a little walking. Rough walking? Yes, I said. According to the map.

We were packed and away as the late February sun cleared the great hill barrier to the south. Due to coastal crags and the steepness of the shoreline we climbed directly some hundreds of feet until from a vantage we lounged and gazed the length of the loch, tide on the turn but otherwise placid. Ladhar Bheinn rose trailing ridges and blue shadows and the snowy hills beyond were Lunnie Bheinn and Meall Buidhe. At the loch's other end a blueish pall hung over stands of conifers, woodsmoke I reckoned. I felt the sun on my face and sat back and closed my eyes.

Much of the natural woodland was fenced so we scaled into these enclosures and pressed through rank heather and ungrazed grasses and birch saplings and myrtle. A goat on the outside watched our movements. The rough climbing slowed us as did Nick's feet, though he didn't complain. He was out of painkillers. So was I. The path to Barrisdale opposite was a slender scar rising over bluffs and disappearing among pines and I pointed it out to Nick and spoke about our searching for Clive on that winter's day nearly two years before. Outwith the enclosure the woodland was patchy and marked by ancients, full-grown and great trunked and some fallen and ringbarked, no young rising to replace them. On the ground the tiny leaves of celandine hinted that at this level at least spring was near. Oystercatchers and herons seemed oblivious to us. Five grey seals sunning on a rock slumped into the sea as we passed.

With the extra day at the bothy we'd run low on food and I felt weary. There were signs here the coast was more intensively used in the past, holding-pens for beasts and walls set amongst bracken though all broken now and a house a century in ruin. As we dropped again to the shoreline the trees thickened. Old oaks in clefts and the spaces between boulders. There was no apparent way through any of this and I thought folk in the past did as we did and picked their way, our pace poor and no rhythm to it yet the land wild and giving much in return and in any case we had supplies for a last night and planned a last camp.

Around the next headland lay Kinloch Hourn, a little less than two miles away. We pitched atop dead bracken just above the high tide mark and in a small bay that was hardly a bay at all. As the sun dropped behind Ladhar Bheinn and faded from the high ground we went combing the shore for driftwood and returned with a great bundle. Stars gathered in the clear sky and a frost set in, the dead stalks by the tent snapping when walked on. We built up the fire and sat in its warmth and spoke of our friend and in a place where he was lost. I said there would always be a space by the fire in case he showed in whatever guise, for he was a conjurer of sorts, a shaper of lives. The salt wood burned orange and blue. The falling sound of a waterfall coming from the darkness beyond. Later I took my bivouac outside and lay under Polaris as Clive loved to do, but it was way too cold, and went back inside and zipped myself in.

At some hour of night the stars vanished from the sky and there was no light anywhere. A cold wind ferreted in from the east, from the head of the loch. By morning it had taken away the frost and brought dense clouds to the surrounding peaks and it was darker than the time suggested. A grey and cold day in the making. I thought there would be snow before it was out.

A few weeks after the big search I'd teamed with a close friend of Clive and her husband for another visit to Knoydart. This time we walked to Kinloch Hourn Lodge, through the exotic woodland, heading east then north along the line of Allt Coire Sgoresdail. I didn't think we'd find anything as this land had been gone over many times already. It was part search, part pilgrimage. Only a little water ran over the small falls and collected in crystal pools and mirrored the dry country. A bleached land after months of winter, the high peaks still holding large snowfields and cornices overhanging the cliffs like grotesque fungi, pure white in the sunshine. At times and especially when blocks of rock obscured our view we descended to the burn and poked among the pools. There'd not been a spate or even a decent flow in weeks. A rocky step took us high to a lovely hanging valley at a thousand feet and we stepped over the burn again. The waters meandered quietly and nudged the path which we could see begin to climb to a pass pinched by rock-strewn slopes. There didn't seem much point in continuing. We sat down for lunch. Before we turned back Clive's friend set some flowers by a rock then pulled from her daysac a small packet of fishfingers and placed them next to the flowers. She said she'd once witnessed a hungry Clive in his flat after a night out attempting to thaw the breaded sticks in his toaster. The room filled with smoke and the charred fingers went into the bin.

I kicked over the cold ash of last night's fire and packed and on slippery rocks we crossed the burn fed by the waterfall and crossed a raised beach to a small headland. By ledges and rocksteps we footed a little above the shoreline, the coast falling away steeply and eventually sheer and forcing us to climb. We could see the flats of Kinloch Hourn but the shore route looked impassable, bluffs and small drops into the sea and all crowded with wild growing birch. Hanging onto branches and trunks we pulled up through the wood to a fine path which a long time ago had been hacked from the slope. The path to the lodge. A cold wind swirled and the air clammy as a cave and like yesterday we smelt burning wood. The path lost height and regained the shoreline where we trod salt turf and tidewrack and drifted past piles of freshly-cut rhododendron. The small additions Victorian gardeners made to their plots now out of control. Such a pile smouldering further up the slope and dense smoke streamed westwards and in the dark groves a man in a yellow jacket dragging something. I don't think he saw us.

When we stepped from the tree cover the wind hit us and for a second I buckled, surprised at its strength. An east wind on your underbelly, born of the land and squeezed to a bottleneck by the Quoich corridor and falling and squeezed again to deliver a great punch where the river meets sea. A vanguard of sleet on its wings and we had to stop and pull on our shell trousers and overmitts and tighten our hoods. Dressed for the summits. Dark cloud spilled from the hillsides and snow and sleet falling against them. Darker now than it was this morning. Dark of the north coast and colder too. We came to the river.

It is true a part of me didn't want him found, his grave to be always in this mighty arena, more beautiful than any words written. I thought the mountains would never release him but they did eventually. He had lain in the pool through frigid April days and through the rain of May, for it was wet that month, the pool now deep enough for speckled trout who slowed in their turning and dippers nested sure he wouldn't wake and frogs hoofed over him and larvae hatched in the eddy of his arms. On the watered banks a bloom of tormentil, stitchwort, bedstraw, the new birch canopy casting over the pool a mottled and trembling shade. One day a storm in the hills sent down a spate which lifted and carried him as if destined for the sea's clemency, only to be caught and seen by the farmer and taken home.

I stood and bent and touched the soft ground and watched the snow fall. Falling and melting. All the wide world narrowed here. To the sound of water.

Acknowledgements

I am grateful to Gordon Robertson of Assynt Foundation for his openness in answering my queries. I would also like to thank Gordon Sleight for his help in my research of land-use and placenames around Loch Assynt.